SERIES EDITOR: TONY HOLMES

OSPREY AIRCRAFT OF THE ACES® • 57

Hurricane Aces 1941-45

Andrew Thomas

OSPREY
PUBLISHING

Front Cover
Among the units sent to reinforce the meagre RAF resources in Burma after the outbreak of war in the region in December 1941 was No 135 Sqn. The unit was commanded by one of the RAF's leading fighter pilots, Sqn Ldr Frank Carey, and initially flew aircraft from other units. By late January, however, it was established at Mingaladon for the defence of the Burmese capital, Rangoon. Among its many untried pilots was a 27-year-old Australian former school teacher, Plt Off Jack Storey, who had made his first claim on the 29th during his first combat sortie.

The Japanese were regularly raiding Rangoon and the nearby airfield at Mingaladon. Just before 0900 hrs on Friday 6 February 1942, a raid was detected and some Tomahawks from the American Volunteer Group, together with No 135 Sqn, scrambled to intercept. With Carey's aircraft unserviceable on the ground, it was Storey (flying Z5659/WK-C), with Sgt Roberson as his No 2, who led the six Hurricanes. They climbed rapidly into the sun. Ground control told them that the enemy were at high altitude and in great number, but gave no directions. During the climb, two of the Hurricanes lost formation. Passing 16,000 ft, Storey sighted the enemy about six miles to his left and some 5000 ft above. The Japanese formation comprised 25 highly-manoeuvrable Ki-27 'Nate' (Army Type 97) fighters of the veteran 50th and 77th *Sentais*.

Turning his four fighters to the right to get 'up-sun', Storey sighted three of the enemy machines slightly above, attempting to bounce them. He immediately entered a left-hand vertical spiral turn. When 'up-sun', he fired a burst into one of the 'Nates'. A whirling free-for-all then ensued, with the Australian gaining a good position behind one of the Japanese fighters. With a devastating burst of fire, Storey sent it spiralling to its destruction south of Zayatkwin airfield, north-east of Rangoon. As the slower-climbing AVG Tomahawks arrived, he was engaged from behind by two more Ki-27s. Again Storey spiralled left. Ramming his throttle open, he once more swept 'up-sun', before

swooping on them. He made a quarter attack on the rearmost 'Nate' and fired two accurate bursts. It spun to the right and crashed. Storey was again engaged by further Japanese fighters but he evaded them. By this stage his engine was overheating. He fired on two more 'Nates', which he believed he had hit, although he did not observe the results. His ammunition exhausted, Storey managed to disengage and recover to base. There, just one bullet hole was discovered in his wing – although

his spark plugs needed changing! In this epic fight against the odds, Jack Storey was credited with two Ki-27s destroyed and two probables from total RAF claims for three confirmed, three probables and three damaged. Lt Kitamura of the 77th *Sentai* was possibly one of his victims, for he was listed as missing.

This painting by artist Mark Postlethwaite shows Jack Storey's second victim spinning to its destruction as he turns to counter the threat of other Ki-27s closing behind him

First published in Great Britain in 2003 by Osprey Publishing
Elms Court, Chapel Way, Botley, Oxford, OX2 9LP

ISBN 1 84176 610 0

Edited by Tony Holmes and Bruce Hales-Dutton
Page design by Mark Holt
Cover Artwork by Mark Postlethwaite
Aircraft Profiles by John Weal
Scale Drawings by Mark Styling
Index by Alan Thatcher
Printed by Stamford Press PTE, Singapore

03 04 05 06 07   10 9 8 7 6 5 4 3 2 1

EDITOR'S NOTE
To make this best-selling series as authoritative as possible, the Editor would be interested in hearing from any individual who may have relevant photographs, documentation or first-hand experiences relating to the world's elite pilots, and their aircraft, of the various theatres of war. Any material used will be credited to its original source. Please write to Tony Holmes via e-mail at:
tony.holmes@osprey-jets.freeserve.co.uk

For details of all Osprey Publishing titles please contact us at:

Osprey Direct UK, PO Box 140, Wellingborough, Northants NN8 4ZA, UK
E-mail: **info@ospreydirect.co.uk**

**Osprey Direct USA, c/o MBI Publishing, PO Box 1, 729 Prospect Ave,
Osceola, WI 54020, USA**
E-mail: **info@ospreydirectusa.com**

Or visit our website: **www.ospreypublishing.com**

CONTENTS

PROLOGUE

Blue Section had been ordered to patrol the Aberdeen area at 3000 ft. Vectored to intercept an incoming Luftwaffe raid, Flt Lt J A Walker, flying at 'Blue 2', described what happened next;

'Approaching Aberdeen, "Blue 1" sighted the smoke trail of an enemy aircraft coming from the east, which was identified as a Ju 88. We were at 10,000 ft and the enemy aircraft was at about 4000-5000 ft above. "Blue 1" attacked first and was hit by return fire, followed by "Blue 3". The enemy aircraft then went into cloud. When it reappeared I was above it at 5000 ft and fired at extreme range and it went back into cloud. "Blue 3" closed again and the enemy aircraft was last seen at 2500 ft travelling slowly and losing height 70 miles south-east of Montrose, with both engines emitting black smoke, glycol and oil splashing out and the undercarriage was also dropped.'

It was just after 1300 hrs on New Year's Day 1941 when the seven-victory ace 'Johnnie' Walker of No 111 Sqn claimed a Junkers Ju 88 as probably destroyed. It was a claim he shared with the rest of Blue Section, Sqn Ldr Biggar and Plt Off Kellett.

Walker had been flying a Hurricane I (P3106), an aircraft type which No 111 Sqn had flown with distinction since it became the first unit to operate the Hawker fighter some three years earlier. Since then the Hurricane had formed the backbone of RAF Fighter Command during the Battle of Britain (see *Osprey Aircraft of the Aces 18 - Hurricane Aces 1939-40*). Now, at the start of 1941, it was still equipping no fewer than 39 fighter squadrons in the UK. However, several units had been recently formed and were still working up. The re-equipment of others with Spitfires was imminent. Nonetheless, further squadrons formed for service in Britain and abroad through 1941.

At the turn of the year six overseas-based squadrons were flying Hurricanes – No 261 was in Malta, 33, 73 and 274 were in Egypt, while in the Sudan and Kenya, respectively, were Nos 1 and 3 Sqns of the South African Air Force. That the Hurricane was still needed is evident from this

At the start of 1941 many Battle of Britain aces were still commanding frontline fighter squadrons, among them Sqn Ldr Bob Stanford Tuck of No 257, who is seen taxiing V6864/DT-A for the press in January 1941 (*J D Oughton*)

Sgt Alfred Marshall of No 73 Sqn flies his favourite Hurricane I V7562/TP-A along the coast near Sollum in January 1941. He became an ace on 3 January when he shot down three SM.79s. Marshall destroyed another near Gambut in this aircraft two days later, and he was also flying it on 9 April when he shot down a Ju 52/3m over Derna (*D Minterne*)

Hurricane I V7474/A (closest to the camera) was flown by Flt Lt J A F Maclachlan of No 261 Sqn when he claimed the first victories scored over Malta in 1941 on 9 January. Another notable pilot to fly this particular aircraft was Sgt Harry Ayre, who shot down a Ju 87 with it ten days later (*P H Barker*)

plea contained in a combat report written by Plt Off Peter Turnbull, then flying Gladiators with No 3 Sqn RAAF, 'please, Father Christmas, send me a Hurricane'. It was a squadron joke, but at length the Hurricanes did arrive. Turnbull, who was to become an ace, called his *Ortogo*.

In North Africa the first Libyan campaign against the Italians was at its height. On 1 January No 258 Wing was formed to control the fighter squadrons in the desert, and Hurricanes were soon in action. Sgt Alfred Marshall of No 73 Sqn already had 3.5 victories to his credit. He opened the RAF's desert account for 1941 on 3 January in a skilful action against five Savoia-Marchetti SM.79s he discovered attacking the monitor HMS *Terror* off Bardia. He wrote;

'At 300 yards I fired my first burst. Within half a minute one of the Savoias had caught fire and was plunging into the sea. I turned to attack another and saw two of the crew bale out as my fire was again successful. The third got it in the starboard motor and the aircraft went into a long glide which finished in the Mediterranean. I silenced the return fire from the fourth Savoia and pieces of metal flew off to starboard. There was little chance of her ever making base. It was a pity my ammunition ran out as the fifth was a sitter.'

Marshall's outstanding combat made him the first Hurricane pilot to become an ace in 1941.

Over the beleaguered island of Malta the Hurricanes of No 261 Sqn were also soon in action, the unit's first combats coming on 9 January when Macchi C.200s of 6° *Gruppo* attacked Luqa. They were engaged by

five Hurricanes, including V7474/A flown by Flt Lt James Maclachlan, who reported;

'I saw the formation of enemy aircraft about 10,000 ft below us and five miles to port. As I drew closer, however, I realised they were Macchi 200 fighters, so did a normal astern attack on the right-hand man of the second section of three. I opened fire at about 200 yards and saw most of the burst go into the Macchi. He did a steep diving turn to the right, but I managed to follow and give him two more full deflection squirts while in the turn. The first just missed his tail, but I think most of the second squirt got him. Suddenly, to my amazement, the pilot baled out and I nearly hit his half-opened parachute as it disappeared under my nose.'

Another Macchi also fell to Maclachlan's fire. They were to be the first two of his eventual total of 16.5 victories.

In the Sudan and Kenya, too, the South African Hurricanes were active, No 3 Sqn flying in support of the Imperial offensive which opened from Kenya on the 14th and was followed in the north by an assault on Eritrea three days later. There, Hurricanes of No 1 Sqn SAAF were kept busy escorting RAF Wellesley bombers. The first Italian aircraft fell on the 22nd when a Caproni Ca.133 was shot down.

Within Fighter Command, however, 1941 was to see the Hurricane largely supplanted in the day fighter role by the Spitfire. Nonetheless, many squadrons continued to fly them as day fighters, in the hazardous fighter-bomber role, as single seat nightfighters and, very successfully, as night intruders. Some of the squadrons comprised men who were exiles from occupied European countries, while others belonged to Commonwealth air forces, but most units tended to be multi-national in composition. In 1941, however, it was in overseas theatres that the Hurricane was to become the pre-eminent RAF fighter, both in the Mediterranean and in Africa, while the following year Hurricane squadrons were to encounter a new enemy – the burgeoning might of Japan.

Hurricane pilots would face much hard air fighting over the next few years, and many of them would become aces.

There are new and old faces – as well as several aces – present among this group of No 253 Sqn pilots seen here at Kenley in January 1941. Standing under the propeller is Flg Off 'Shag' Eckford (final total nine destroyed and three shared), fourth from right is the CO, Sqn Ldr P W Walker (three and two shared) and on his right is Flt Lt Myles Duke-Wooley (four and three shared) (*No 253 Sqn Records*)

OFFENCE AND DEFENCE

By early 1941 the Luftwaffe was still recovering from the Battle of Britain and had switched to night raids. But the RAF chose to go on the offensive, Fighter Command initiating a series of offensive missions across the Channel. They were known as *Circuses* and *Rhubarbs*, *Circuses* being flown by a few bombers with fighter support, while *Rhubarbs* were undertaken by pairs of fighters. Inflicting only modest damage on the enemy, they soon, however, began to take their toll of some of the command's most able pilots.

The first *Circus,* to Guines aerodrome near Calais, was flown on 12 January 1941, with part of the escort being provided by No 242 Sqn, led by Flt Lt Stan Turner. Two days later No 242 mounted its first *Rhubarb* under its inspirational CO, the legless Sqn Ldr Douglas Bader. He and Turner headed low over the Channel for France, and half way across attacked a pair of E-boats and a converted trawler. Although exhilarating, these attacks turned out to be extremely hazardous. Later in the day, Flt Off Willie McKnight (in P2961/LE-A) and another pilot attacked ground targets along the coast. McKnight, the squadron's leading ace with 17 and two shared destroyed and three unconfirmed destroyed, probably fell to anti-aircraft fire, as did 7.5 victory ace Flg Off John Latta in V7203/LE-T soon afterwards. In just one day, therefore, the squadron had lost two experienced pilots for little return.

During a *Rhubarb* in early February another future ace, the Czech Sgt Karel Kuttelwascher of No 1 Sqn, made his first claim as a member of the

The first ace to fall in 1941 was No 242 Sqn's fiery Canadian Flg Off Willie McKnight, who was lost on one of the first *Rhubarbs* on 12 January in P2961/LE-A. This machine wore his dramatic personal marking, inspired by McKnight's pre-war medical studies in Canada (*G R Pitchfork*)

Lost on a *Rhubarb* at the same time as Willie McKnight was 7.5-victory ace Plt Off John Latta, who was flying No 242 Sqn Hurricane V7203/LE-T (*G R Pitchfork*)

RAF, while at the same time the first squadron of American volunteers, No 71 'Eagle' Sqn, became operational.

Despite the increase in offensive activity, Fighter Command's priority remained the defence of Britain against air attack, and although the emphasis had switched to night bombing, there were still regular intrusions by day. On 8 February Turner and two others scrambled in cloud and intercepted an all black Do 17 off Clacton. Turner's fire destroyed its right wing and fuselage and made one engine smoke. The kill was shared by all three pilots, and represented Turner's last with the Hurricane.

By now improved Hurricane IIs were appearing in greater numbers, No 242 Sqn re-equipping during February. Shortly afterwards Bader was promoted and replaced by Sqn Ldr Paddy Treacy, who shared a Ju 88 on 1 April to become an ace. But he was to have little time to enjoy his new status as during a sweep on the 20th he collided with two other aircraft and all three pilots died. In a disastrous month, No 242 lost three other pilots, including Flt Lt Hugh Tamblyn, who had 5.5 victories.

The Luftwaffe was encountered all round the UK coast, including the Irish Sea. One such intruder was caught by a detachment from the Czech-manned No 312 Sqn at

Flt Sgt Otmar Kucera (right) and two Czech colleagues of No 312 Sqn pose by his Hurricane IIB (Z3437/DU-K) at Kenley at about the time that he used it to probably destroy a Bf 109 off Gravelines on 18 June 1941 (*Z Hurt*)

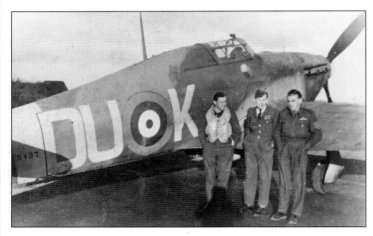

Flt Sgt Otmar Kucera sits in Z3437/DU-K, which displays the kill marking denoting his first 'solo' victory – a Bf 109 on 3 July 1941 – although on that occasion he was flying Z3314 (which he also used to claim a second Bf 109 destroyed six days later) (*Z Hurt*)

Penrhos on 14 March, and Flt Lt Dawbarn led Sgt Josef Stehlik in pursuit of the German bomber, as the latter reported;

'I sighted an aircraft approaching on the starboard bow at about 330 degrees. The aircraft was about 1000 ft below us. I recognised it as a Ju 88, carrying out a converging attack. This attack was carried out by my section leader from the right side, and I followed him 15 yards from the left side. I opened fire at about 200 yards for three seconds. During this attack there was return fire from the rear gun of the Ju 88. After that the enemy aircraft was seen to dive slightly and I repeated my quarter attacks. On the third attack, just above sea level, I noticed that the starboard engine had ceased to function, and I could see oil coming from it. After the last attack I saw the enemy aircraft land in the water with the tail broken off. The aircraft remained visible in the sea for about 20 seconds, then tipped up onto its nose and disappeared under the water 20 seconds later.'

On 24 March days another exiled airman was in action off Hastings, on the south coast, during a convoy escort. 'Moses' Demozay of No 1 Sqn, in Z2484, spotted a Bf 109 diving out of the clouds, and the subsequent fight is described in the squadron history;

'A '109 came down and, warned by his No 2, Demozay took violent evasive action. Then two '109s attacked from astern. The Frenchman throttled back and they overshot him and went into low cloud. Following them, he emerged right behind the two fighters and fired at one with a long 12-second burst. The '109 burst into flames and went down.'

The first of Demozay's 18 victories was also No 1's first with the Hurricane II.

Some day fighter squadrons were also required to mount night sorties on occasion, especially in areas of the country less vulnerable to attack. In Northern Ireland, No 245 Sqn had yet to see much action. It was commanded by Sqn Ldr John Simpson, who had 6.5 victories from his time with No 43 Sqn in 1940. Early on 8 April he scrambled

Below and bottom
Hurricane I W9200/DX-? was the aircraft of Sqn Ldr John Simpson, who led No 245 Sqn at Aldergrove. He used this aircraft to shoot down an He 111 of III./KG 26 on the night of 7/8 April 1941. A month later, on 5/6 May, Simpson was again flying this machine when he downed a second night raider (believed to have been yet another He 111, this time from II./KG 40). The aircraft is seen just after the May victory, with the scoreboard suitably updated

in his personal aircraft, W9200/DX-?, and spotted the enemy west of Down Patrick, as he recorded at the time;

'When at 6500 ft I sighted two black objects about 800 ft above me, flying north-west. I climbed to investigate, and when 500 ft below and behind I recognised them as aircraft. Still climbing, both aircraft opened fire on me, their shooting passing my left wing. I broke away, climbing to the right, and lost sight of the aircraft. I turned left, my height now being 9000 ft, and saw two aircraft flying north-west 1500 ft below me, clearly silhouetted against the white cloud. I crept down and opened fire at about 200 yards on the No 2. My gun flashes dazzled me and I broke away slightly right. Still seeing the aircraft, I came in again to attack the No 2.

'The enemy aircraft were travelling very slowly at about 130 mph. I closed to about 100 yards and opened fire, slightly right of the astern position. Return fire passed over me and stopped after one second. I closed to 80 yards and fired again. The aircraft was now diving, and attacking was made easier. My bullets were striking the centre section and right wing. I was slightly below, and felt no slipstream. There was a large black bump under the centre section in front of the lower gondola, approximately between the engines, which protruded below the lower gun position. I continued to fire, closing to 50 yards, and a red glow appeared above this black object. Still firing, there was almost immediately a very violent explosion which threw my aircraft approximately 300 ft into the air and on its side. I saw that the enemy aircraft had exploded, and pieces of burning aircraft were falling to the sea. As I was thrown by this explosion, a large white object narrowly missed my left wing. I then retuned to base.'

Simpson's eighth kill is thought to have been a He 111 of III./KG 26.

On the other side of the UK, early May saw another day fighter unit, No 43 Sqn, enjoy a successful period of night action. Based at Drem for the defence of Edinburgh and the Forth anchorages, it was led by Battle of Britain ace Sqn Ldr Tommy Dalton-Morgan. He took off in Z3150/FT-V late on 5 May, and at midnight, over Anstruther, sighted a Ju 88 2000 ft beneath him. He reported;

'I made a left hand turn, closed to 400 ft range dead astern and opened fire. Observing no effect from this fire, I closed to 100 ft and gave another burst. There was a violent explosion which flung my aircraft upwards and to one side, and I saw pieces of the enemy aircraft flying through the air.'

Dalton-Morgan landed 25 minutes later, refuelled and was off again before 0130 hrs. Having been up for 20 minutes, he spotted another bomber near Fife Ness;

'I climbed to attack and it opened fire, but to no effect. I closed to 150 yards dead astern and gave three short bursts, and the enemy aircraft dived into cloud with the port engine on fire. Following it through the cloud, I gave two more short bursts, and when 500 ft above the

Scrambling from Drem in Hurricane I Z3150/FT-V on the night of 5/6 May 1941, Sqn Ldr Tommy Dalton-Morgan brought down two German bombers off the Firth of Forth – his tenth and eleventh victories (*M C Cotton*)

Seen after the award of a bar to his DFC, No 43 Sqn's CO, Sqn Ldr Tommy Dalton-Morgan, poses beneath an aggressive version of the unit's 'fighting cock' badge (*M C Cotton*)

Hurricane I V6997/JX-H of No 1 Sqn was regularly flown by Czech ace Sgt Josef Dygryn during January and February 1941. All five of the enemy aircraft he destroyed were claimed with the unit in May and June of that year. Posted to No 310 'Czech' Sqn in September 1941, Dygryn returned to No 1 Sqn in mid-May 1942, and was lost in action (almost certainly hit by flak) over Le Havre on 4 June. His body was eventually washed ashore at Worthing, on the south coast, on 8 September (*No 1 Sqn Records*)

water there was a violent flash which immediately went out as the enemy aircraft crashed into the sea.'

He was credited with two destroyed that night. The following night Dalton-Morgan was airborne again, and soon after 0100 hrs on the 7th he found another bomber approaching from the west. It was to become his 12th victory, and another 3.5 would come during the summer.

Meanwhile, No 43 Sqn's Belgian flight commander, Flt Lt Leroy Du Vivier, was also in on the action that same night. Performing a practice flight, he and his wingman were ordered to the east of St Abbs Head. There, they encountered a Ju 88, which was promptly sent into the sea. This shared kill was Du Vivier's second success, and No 43's sixth within five days – no mean achievement for a 'day fighter' squadron. Late in the month a more sombre task fell to the squadron when it was detached to Prestwick, Scotland, to cover the return of the damaged battleship HMS *Prince of Wales* after its encounter with the *Bismarck*. From there on the 28th Du Vivier scrambled to intercept a reconnaissance Ju 88 from 2(F)./ObdL, which he brought down with two of the crew dead.

Further south, No 1 Sqn also mounted nocturnal operations as German night raids on London reached a peak. On 10/11 May Moses Demozay brought down a Heinkel caught in the searchlights. Soon afterwards it was the turn of the Czech Sgt Josef Dygryn. At 17,000 ft over the capital, flying Z2687, he spotted a twin-engined bomber flying parallel and just below him. Its gunner fired at him but stopped when Dygryn opened fire, and he duly followed the Heinkel down as it fell to earth. After refuelling, Dygryn was off again, and over Kenley he saw He 111 'A1+CL' of 3./KG 53 above him, heading south. Giving chase, he opened fire and saw smoke. It increased until the bomber burst into flames and spun in. Not content with these successes, the Czech pilot was

On 19 May 1941 No 87 Sqn sent a detachment to the Scilly Isles. Although Hurricane I P2798/LK-A was the usual aircraft of Sqn Ldr 'Widge' Gleed, it was used by Plt Off Ivor Badger when he shot down an Ar 196 soon after the unit's arrival (*No 87 Sqn Records*)

Plt Off Ivor Badger enjoys a well-earned brew outside No 87 Sqn's dispersal hut at St Mary's soon after shooting down an Arado Ar 196 floatplane and dramatically claiming the detachment's first victory (*R F Watson*)

north-east of Biggin Hill when, at 0315 hrs he found a Ju 88 flying at 16,000 ft. Closing to point blank range, he fired all his ammunition in several bursts, and the bomber went down trailing smoke. It eventually crashed into the sea off Hastings. The squadron CO, Sqn Ldr 'Boy' Brooker, also brought down a Heinkel, but after its night successes No 1 went back to its day job, Josef Dygryn bringing down a Bf 109 over Tenterden, Kent, for his fourth victory.

Further west, dedicated nightfighter unit No 87 Sqn was having a frustrating time. Its energetic CO, Sqn Ldr 'Widge' Gleed, proposed sending a detachment to the Scilly Isles to counter German anti-shipping and reconnaissance patrols. He led six all-black Hurricanes to the tiny strip on St Mary's late on 19 May, and among the pilots was Plt Off Ivor Badger. Soon after arriving, he scrambled in Gleed's Hurricane, P2798/LK-A. Back within 15 minutes, Badger's laconic handwritten report described what happened;

'Took off at 2100 hrs on signal from AA battery. Enemy aircraft sighted about five miles south of base. Enemy aircraft saw me, dropped its load and headed due south, taking evasive action by turning left and right and swish tailing. Closed aircraft to 200 yards and gave three-second burst from astern. Fired three more bursts, closing to 50 yards. Enemy aircraft did steep turn to right and I broke away above. Enemy aircraft dived into sea and broke up. No survivors seen. Landed at 2115 hrs.'

Badger's victim was Arado Ar 196A-4 '6W+EN' of 5./BFlGr, flown by Oberfelwebel Günther Nowak in support of *Bismarck's* run towards Brest. Five days later Gleed shared a Do 18 flying boat, having chased it across St Mary's at a few hundred feet and brought it down just off the coast. The small detachment eventually claimed six aircraft destroyed.

— LEANING ACROSS THE CHANNEL —

As the summer approached, Luftwaffe activity fell away as the RAF made increasing incursions into France and Belgium. The American-manned No 71 'Eagle' Sqn also made its mark at last following months of training. In a violent combat during a sweep near Lille on 2 July, the squadron claimed its first kills in the shape of three Bf 109s, one of which fell to Minneapolis-born Plt Off W R Dunn in Z3781. Four days later, west of Merville, Bill Dunn was escorting bombers on a *Circus* when he shared in

the probable destruction of another aircraft. He later commented, 'he probably baled out, but I didn't see him do so'. Flying Z3781 again on the 21st, Dunn shot down another Bf 109F to score his second confirmed victory. His third followed on 9 August at 1130 hrs west of Mardyck. This was his final claim with the Hurricane, but soon afterwards he became the war's first American ace. The second 'Eagle' squadron, No 121, had its first combat on 8 August when future ace Plt Off Sel Edner shared a Ju 88 probable north-east of Hull. It was his only Hurricane claim.

The Polish Hurricane units also made a big contribution to these early sweeps, with South Wales-based No 317 'Wilenski' Sqn flying a mission on 10 July. One of the pilots involved was Sgt Stanislaw Brzeski, who shared a Bf 109 with Flt Lt Szczesny, as Brzeski's combat report recounts;

'About 1.5 miles north of Le Havre I saw an Me 109 at 1000 ft attacking our formation. He passed near, and there was no exchange of fire. Being in formation I saw another Me 109 attacking one of our aircraft in front of me, Flt Lt Szczesny. The enemy aircraft fired without result. Flt Lt Szczesny fired three short bursts from starboard astern. After firing I saw white smoke. I gave boost, and passing my leader's aircraft, attacked from the same side at 250 yards. One long burst of about five seconds and the Me 109 banked steeply and dived into the sea.'

This was No 317's first victory and Szczesny's eighth. Four days later the same pair accounted for a Ju 88 off the South Wales coast near Tenby. It was 23-year-old Brzeski's fifth victory, having already counted an observation balloon destroyed over his homeland in September 1939. His fifth aircraft claim came in December while flying a Spitfire.

Increasingly, however, Spitfires provided the escorts, so some Hurricane squadrons switched to fighter-bomber and anti-shipping duties. One such outfit to make the swap was No 615 Sqn, a veteran Hurricane unit led by Sqn Ldr Denys Gillam, who had 7.5 victories to his

The second American-manned unit to see combat, No 121 'Eagle' Sqn engaged the enemy for the first time on 8 August 1941 when two of its Hurricanes probably destroyed a Ju 88 off Hull. One of the aircraft involved in this action was Z3127/AV-R, flown by future five-victory ace Plt Off Sel Edner from San Jose, California. This would be his only Hurricane claim (*Eagle Association*)

Hurricane I V7339/JH-X was flown by Sgt Stanislaw Brzeski, who was a member of the Polish-manned No 317 Sqn. He was flying the aircraft on a sweep when he shared in the destruction of a Bf 109, which in turn represented the squadron's first victory (*via W Matusiak*)

Hurricane IIA Z2703/KW-M of No 615 'County of Surrey' Sqn was appropriately named *Croydon* – it is seen at the unit's Kenley base in April 1941. On the evening of 18 March, the CO, Sqn Ldr Tony Eyre, was flying the aircraft on a patrol off Dungeness when he spotted two Bf 109s off Hawkinge. They were already diving for home by then, however, and the German fighters could not be caught. The pilot posing in the Hurricane's cockpit is Flg Off Dennis Crowley-Milling, a veteran of the Battle of Britain (*J D R Rawlings collection*)

Five-victory ace Sqn Ldr David Haysom, CO of No 79 Sqn (in Z3745/NV-B), leads Flg Off 'Bee' Beamont (in Z2633/NV-M), who had at that stage accumulated 4.5 of his eventual total of 6.5 victories. These aircraft were photographed whilst on a traning flight from Fairwood Common in the late summer of 1941 (*No 79 Sqn Records*)

name, and counted five-victory ace Flt Lt 'Dutch' Hugo as a flight commander. Channel operations continued through the winter, and although several squadrons were posted overseas during the autumn, others were formed to replace them.

Although the Hurricane was now considered outdated for fighter work, some units continued to fly them into 1942, including No 43 at Acklington, now led by Sqn Ldr Du Vivier. This unit saw occasional action, as its diary for 25 April recounts;

'Squadron Leader du Vivier recognised a Ju 88. Fire was opened from a range of 400 yards with a series of short bursts from the port quarter to astern. The enemy aircraft returned fire and Sqn Ldr du Vivier received superficial skin wounds on the face and neck. The Ju 88 was seen to crash into the sea after one member of the crew had baled out.'

It was du Vivier's fifth and last kill, and made him No 43's latest ace.

The fighter-bomber units saw little air combat, although No 175 Sqn at Warmwell, in Dorset, was busy. Flt Lt Andrew Humphrey with five victories was 'B' Flight CO. Flying BE668, he later recalled scoring No 175's sole victories of the war, on 9 May;

'I sighted six enemy aircraft flying north 500 yards on the port side in three sections of two, the bottom section being Me 109F bombers flying at about 100 ft. I increased speed from 160 to 180 mph and attacked the starboard bomber from below and astern at about 100 yards, closing to 50 yards, giving a two-second burst and allowing about 50 mph for deflection. This enemy aircraft immediately flew into the water on a left-hand diving turn and disappeared. The remaining enemy aircraft then proceeded to attack me from all directions. I continued to fly as low as possible, relying on steep turns to avoid being shot down. All except one of the enemy aircraft seemed content to fly low and attempt to out turn me. The remaining enemy aircraft climbed to about 500 ft and made repeated diving attacks. After about five to ten minutes of dogfighting in this manner, without being able to get a shot at anyone, I got a steady sight on

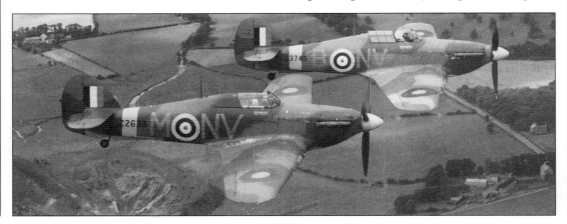

one of the starboard Bf 109Fs which was doing a spiral dive at about 100 ft. After about one second of firing, this enemy aircraft suddenly straightened out of his turn and attempted to pull out of the dive but hit the water very flatly and bounced off the water up to about 30 ft, and then dived straight in. After this the remaining enemy aircraft broke off the engagement.'

Humphrey later rose to become Chief of the Air Staff, and he was the last fighter ace to hold this position.

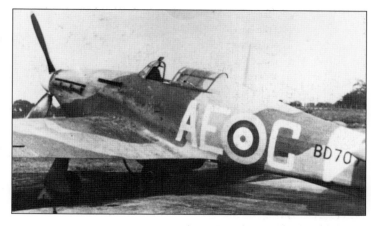

NIGHT HUNTERS

In October 1940 two successful Hurricane squadrons, Nos 85 and 151, were ordered to train for nightfighting duties and to be operational by the turn of the year. Additionally, the pioneer Hurricane nightfighter unit, No 422 Flt, was expanded to form No 96 Sqn. Along with the other fighter units, it flew against the Luftwaffe's night blitz on Britain's cities, which opened in late 1940 and continued through the winter. Given favourable conditions, the single-seaters could be effective, and this was demonstrated during the night of 15/16 January 1941 over London by No 151 Sqn. Plt Off R P Stevens spotted the enemy soon after midnight;

'I was vectored south, and the enemy was reported approaching from starboard. Continuing my vectors, I saw shell bursts at 19,000 ft. I then observed aircraft above and gave chase eastwards and aircraft climbed away to about 30,000 ft, leaving condensation trails from 25,000 ft up. I closed in behind and below, making use of cover from condensation streams. At 25 yards I swung out and delivered a quarter attack. No return fire was experienced, and shots were seen striking the engine centre section and fuselage.

'The enemy aircraft then dived very steeply down to 3000 ft. I followed, and the enemy aircraft then pulled up and I gave one short burst at approximately beam attack at the same time. The aircraft burst properly into flames and crashed in a wood just outside Hornchurch village.'

Richard Stevens' first victory was a Do 17Z of 4./KG 3. Over east London just before 0500 hrs, he was airborne again in V6934/DZ-Y and found an He 111 of 2./KG 53. He brought it down near Southend.

The second unit to switch to night work was No 85 Sqn, which also began scoring during the month. Its first night victory was claimed by its CO, Wg Cdr Peter Townsend, who shot down Do 17Z 'U5+PM' of 4./KG 2 near Sudbury, north-west of London, but as the squadron

On 18 September 1941, Flt Sgt Graham Robertson of No 402 Sqn RCAF used this Hurricane IIB (BD707/AE-C) to probably destroy a Bf 109 in an engagement fought out over the Channel off Beachy Head (*Neville Franklin*)

All-black Hurricane I V6931/DZ-D of No 151 Sqn wears the New Zealand fern leaf decoration chosen by its regular pilot, Kiwi Flt Lt I S 'Black' Smith. The ace made his first night claim – and his last flying the Hurricane – in this aircraft during the Blitz on 10/11 May 1941, when he was credited with an He 111 probably destroyed (*No 151 Sqn Records*)

diary noted, 'the fact that the Dornier left its lights on helped considerably'. It was the last of Townsend's 11 victories.

After a period of sick leave, Richard Stevens began scoring again in April, becoming an ace on the 10th when he shot down a Ju 88 of II./KG 1. His tersely-written combat report takes up the story;

'At 2343 hrs a Ju 88 was sighted ten miles north-east of Banbury at 16,000 ft, flying south. An astern attack was made. Bits of the enemy aircraft flew off and the Hurricane was covered in oil – no return fire. The enemy aircraft dived vertically, but a further burst was fired from astern before the enemy aircraft crashed in a field, which was covered with the burning wreckage. I landed at Wittering at 0024 hrs.'

Airborne again two hours later for a free-lance patrol, he spotted an He 111 at 0230 hrs, which he downed over Kettering. Stevens claimed regularly, but not without risk, as No 151's diary for 13 June reveals;

'Plt Off Stevens intercepted an He 111 over London. He was flying one of the four-cannon Hurricanes and opened fire at 300 yards. The enemy aircraft blew up and nearly wrecked Plt Off Stevens's aircraft.'

By then Stevens was the RAF's leading nightfighter pilot.

There were Hurricanes flying with other nightfighter units, as most, like No 151 Sqn, operated them alongside Boulton-Paul Defiants. One was No 255 Sqn at Hibaldstow, near Lincoln. Finding and engaging an elusive foe in the dark without any radar was never easy, as future night ace Sgt Philip Kendall of No 255 discovered when he attacked a bomber near Humanby, Yorkshire. His frustration is evident from his report;

'I dived, turning to port at the same time to intercept him, and when 600 yards away, fired. Simultaneously, a single searchlight exposed at 90-degrees to starboard. Unfortunately this illuminated me and, as I was diving at the same angle as the beam of the searchlight, I was blinded by its glare and the enemy aircraft made its escape.'

The number of raids fell dramatically through the summer, by which time the more capable Beaufighter was becoming available. Richard Stevens' last victory was on 22 October when he shared in the destruction of an He 111 with a Defiant over the Midlands. He was subsequently lost during an intruder mission in December, by which time he had claimed 14.5 kills at night in Hurricanes – an extraordinary achievement.

IN THE ENEMY'S BACKYARD

Another way of countering the enemy's night bombing offensive was to send intruders over Luftwaffe bomber bases, and several Hurricane units were dedicated to this role for a time, with the most successful being No 1 Sqn. The unit was commanded at the time by Sqn Ldr J A F Maclachlan, who had gained eight victories over Malta prior to losing his left forearm to a cannon shell from a Bf 109 on 16 February 1941.

No 1 began its intrusions on the night of 1 April 1942 when Flt Lt Karel Kuttelwascher headed into France in his soot-black Hurricane IIC BE581/JX-E. Over Melun airfield, the Czech, later christened the 'Night Hawk', spotted a Ju 88 taking off. Closing to 100 yards behind it, he opened fire. The starboard engine was hit and the Ju 88 dived into the ground to achieve No 1's first victory since the previous June. But Kuttelwascher had not finished. Diving, he strafed a Ju 88 on the runway before returning home to begin an astonishing run of success for the

The most successful Czech pilot, and the RAF's foremost single-seat intruder pilot, was Flt Lt Karel Kuttelwascher of No 1 Sqn, who poses here (left) with his armourer on the wing of BE581/JX-E at Tangmere. The five victory symbols shown below the cockpit soon multiplied as he ran up an astonishing series of successes over enemy bomber bases in France during the early summer of 1942 (*Z Hurt*)

squadron during which he destroyed 14 enemy bombers whilst in the landing pattern over their own airfields.

One of the squadron's most successful nights of intruder work came on 3/4 May while Kuttelwascher was operating in the Everaux/St Andre area. Over the latter he spotted six He 111s orbiting and attacked one, setting its starboard engine on fire – the bomber crashed near the airfield. He then turned his attentions to a second bomber, which also fell. A third Heinkel was then shot down. Meanwhile, over Dinard, James Maclachlan, in BD983/JX-G, had missed one bomber but spotted another he thought was a Do 217 with its navigation lights on. Firing from astern, he watched the starboard engine burst into flame before it spun in. He then spotted an He 111 coming in to land, which he fired at until it too fell in flames. The two pilots had got five bombers in one night.

The squadron's run of success was not without cost, however. On the night of 4 June one of its aces from 1941, Czech Wt Off Josef Dygryn DFM, who had recently returned to the unit, was lost in Z3183 during an intruder sortie. It is likely that he fell victim to flak, and his body was later washed ashore on the south coast. No 1 Sqn's period of intruder duty ended on the night of 1 July when Kuttelwascher destroyed two Do 217s near Dinard. The unit withdrew to re-equip with Typhoons soon afterwards. Some Hurricanes still remained with Fighter Command, mainly as 'parasite' fighters for Turbinlight Havocs fitted with radar and searchlights, but the aircraft's time as a fighter over the UK had passed.

ACES OVER THE SEA

A hooked version of the Hurricane was developed for the Royal Navy, and examples were first embarked with 880 Naval Air Squadron (NAS) in HMS *Furious* in July 1941 for the attack on the Arctic port of Petsamo. During this action Lt Cdr F E Judd shot down a Do 18 flying boat to score the Sea Hurricane's first victory, although most engagements involving the aircraft would be in the Mediterranean. This was not the first use of the Hurricane at sea, however.

Due to the Royal Navy's desperate shortage of carriers to perform vital convoy escort duties in the Atlantic, the concept of the catapult fighter had been born in an effort to counter the long-range Fw 200 Condor threat. A Hurricane would be carried on a heavy catapult mounted on the bow of a merchant ship and fired off by rockets when the presence of an intruder was detected. After the interception, the theory was that the pilot would either attempt to reach land or bale out into the sea near an escort ship. Such vessels were designated Catapult Armed Merchantmen, or CAM ships. The Royal Navy also commissioned four Fighter Catapult Ships from February 1941. 804 NAS was assigned to them, although the first operational launch was not until 18 July.

On 3 August Lt Bob Everett was aboard HMS *Maplin*, escorting a convoy from Gibraltar when, in the early afternoon, a Condor was sighted and Everett was launched in Sea Hurricane W9277. He soon spotted the Condor, and in the face of heavy defensive fire, closed to within 200 yards and fired a series of long bursts. This caused the Condor to spew oil and catch fire before it crashed into the sea. Everett then ditched his damaged fighter near to HMS *Wanderer* and was quickly picked up. Bob Everett had claimed the first 'Hurricat' kill, for which he was awarded the DSO.

Paradoxically, it was pilots wearing light blue uniforms who performed the longest CAM ship operations. Some were already aces when they embarked, while others were to reach that status. The Merchant Ship Fighter Unit (MSFU) was formed at Speke on 5 May to man the CAM ship detachments, each vessel having an RAF pilot and groundcrew with a Royal Navy direction officer. The first pilot to arrive was Plt Off Henry Davidson, who joined the first CAM ship, the SS *Empire Rainbow*. An experienced fighter pilot with seven victories from the Battle of Britain, Davidson made the first trial launch on 31 May and sailed with the ship for Halifax on the first operational run by the MSFU on 8 June. Among the other pilots to volunteer for the unit were Battle of Britain aces Flg Offs John Greenwood, who joined *Empire Flame*, 'Spud' Spurdle and 'Stapme' Stapleton.

The first MSFU action came on a return voyage from Halifax when Plt Off Eric Varley launched from *Empire Foam*. He encountered an Fw 200 with its bomb-bay doors open, its crews, who were doubtless horrified to find a fighter in mid-Atlantic, speeding away at low level into cloud. Varley eventually baled out and was picked up. He was later credited with four victories, including two Arado Ar 234 jet bombers.

Both crews and aircraft suffered horribly in the Atlantic winter, and by 1942 CAM ships were also included in convoys to Russia and Gibraltar. It was on the Russian run that the MSFU tasted its first success when, on the morning of 25 May 1942, Flg Off John Kendall, homeward bound in *Empire Morn*, was launched against a shadowing Ju 88, which he downed into the Barents Sea. He baled out too low, however, and died soon after being picked up.

After the disaster of convoy PQ 17 in September 1942, newly-commissioned escort carrier HMS *Avenger* was included to support the next, PQ 18. The vessel carried 12 Sea Hurricanes of 802 and 883 NASs, the former being commanded by Lt E W T Taylour DSC, who had seven victories from his time as a Fulmar I pilot with 808 NAS. From Norway, Luftwaffe bombers attempted to stop the convoy, and on the afternoon of the 13th, 150 miles north west of Bear Island, the attack developed. A huge formation of Ju 88 and He 111 torpedo bombers swept in and eight vessels were sunk. Later, four fighters chased an He 115 floatplane, which escaped after its defensive fire had hit Taylour's Sea Hurricane, sending it down in flames. His loss was avenged on the 14th, however, when fighters broke up the attacks and shot down five bombers.

The MSFU continued on convoy operations, although in diminishing numbers as more escort carriers became available. On 1 November 1942

Flt Lt 'Stapme' Stapleton of No 257 Sqn lets the wind flow through his hair as he flies an all-black Hurricane IIB from High Ercall during the summer of 1942. The Battle of Britain veteran was one of a number of aces from that campaign to volunteer for service with the Merchant Ship Fighter Unit (MSFU) (*via C H Thomas*)

A Sea Hurricane of the MSFU sits on its catapult on a Catapult Armed Merchantman during 1941. Although few victories were scored by these aircraft, the deterrent effect of the CAM-ship fighters on German raiders was significant (*J D Oughton*)

Flg Off Norman Taylor DFM, who had 5.5 victories to his credit, was aboard *Empire Heath* in a returning Gibraltar convoy. He was strapped into V7070 when 'action stations' was sounded – a Condor had been sighted about ten miles away.

Taylor was launched as the bows of the vessel rose in the heavy swell, and just as the enemy had started an attack run on the CAM ship. He turned towards the Condor and chased the now retreating bomber at full throttle. He closed in despite being blinded by the dazzle from the sea and a furious curtain of defensive fire from the Fw 200. His port wing was hit, and the bomber, now flying very low, pulled up in an attempt to reach cloud. Taylor called, 'he's pulled up in front of me. I think I've got him'. Closing to 200 yards, he opened up and his fire hit the Condor's cockpit. It continued to climb, before entering a shallow dive and crashing into the sea. Taylor announced his final kill over the R/T, calling 'He's down. He's gone down'. There was no sign of survivors from 7./KG 40's 'F8+DS', flown by Oberleutnant Arno Gross's crew.

Taylor then flew back to the convoy and baled out, but he was a non-swimmer. Barely able to stay afloat, he was lucky to be picked up. The only ace to claim a kill with the MSFU, he received a well-earned DFC.

In March 1943 the remaining CAM ships were concentrated on the Gibraltar run and the MSFU was officially disbanded on 8 June. However, on 23 July, the last two CAM ships were at sea en route from Gibraltar in convoy SL 133. When attacked by Condors, Sea Hurricanes launched from *Empire Darwin* and *Empire Tide*. They shot down two Fw 200s to ensure that the MSFU had a successful end to its brief existence. But Sea Hurricanes remained operational with several Fleet Air Arm units attached to escort carriers on Atlantic and Arctic convoy duty until finally being replaced by Grumman Wildcats in September 1944.

MURMANSK EXPEDITION

After the German invasion of the Soviet Union in June 1941, Britain offered immediate assistance, and in late July a plan to send a wing of two Hurricane squadrons to north Russia was approved. A flight from No 17 Sqn duly moved to Leconfield to form the nucleus of a new squadron, No 134. One flight commander was the diminutive Flt Lt Jack Ross, who had recently claimed his fifth victory (a shared Ju 88 shot down off Sumburgh). The second unit formed around a flight from No 504 Sqn, which now became No 81. The preparations proceeded swiftly, and some aircraft were loaded on to the carrier HMS *Argus* to be flown off, while others were crated and shipped to the port of Archangel.

Argus arrived at its flying-off point on 7 September, and No 134 Sqn's 'A' Flight was the first off, led by the CO, Sqn Ldr A G Miller, followed by 'A' and 'B' Flights of No 81 Sqn. All landed safely at Vaenga, about ten miles north of Murmansk, in the Soviet Arctic – just a few miles east of the

The diminutive Flt Lt Jack Ross was an established ace who served with No 134 Sqn in Russia, and he conducted much of the instruction of Soviet pilots onto the Hurricane. Here, Ross shows future 16-kill ace Capt Boris Safanov the cockpit drills during a snowstorm (*No 81 Sqn Records*)

The first victory of the RAF's expedition to Russia fell to Flt Sgt 'Wag' Haw of No 81 Sqn, who brought down a Bf 109 near Murmansk in this Hurricane IIB (Z4018/FH-41) on 12 September 1941. He shot down another while flying the same aircraft on the 27th to become the leading RAF pilot in Russia (*No 81 Sqn Records*)

frontline. The following day, the wing's Soviet hosts held a banquet in their honour, as Jack Ross confided to his diary;

'The whole Wing passed out completely after drinking vodka. I was so bad I completely missed the concert given in our honour.'

Both units flew their first patrols on the morning of 11 September. Ross, in Z3763/GY, and 'B' Flight were led by a Russian captain to the Finnish frontier, although no enemy aircraft were encountered. The Luftwaffe was seen the very next day, however, when a patrol from No 134 Sqn sighted some enemy bombers. They could not make contact, although a section from No 81 Sqn damaged a Bf 110. That afternoon No 81's duty section, led by Flt Sgt 'Wag' Haw in Z4018/FH-41, scrambled towards the port of Petsamo, where they sighted five Bf 109Es of I./JG 77 escorting an Hs 126 on a reconnaissance sortie. Haw's combat report describes the encounter;

'The enemy aircraft were approaching from ahead and slightly to the left, and as I turned towards them, they turned slowly to the right. I attacked the leader, and as he turned, I gave him a ten-second burst from the full abeam position. The enemy aircraft rolled onto its back, and as it went down it burst into flames.'

Haw's friend, Sgt 'Ibby' Waud, was more succinct. 'It was an awesome sight, the '109 drifting along inverted with flames and debris pouring from it'. Waud then attacked the Henschel, which he downed in flames – the second of his four kill. Sgt 'Nudger' Smith was shot down, however, and he would be the only pilot to die on the expedition.

Patrols continued on a daily basis, and an evening escort to Pe 2 bombers near Balucha five days later was bounced by two prowling Bf 109s. The first was hit by several Hurricanes, caught fire and crashed. The second was chased by Haw, who later wrote;

'Two Me 109s dived over and passed in front of us. I attacked the second as he turned and dived westwards. I made an astern attack from

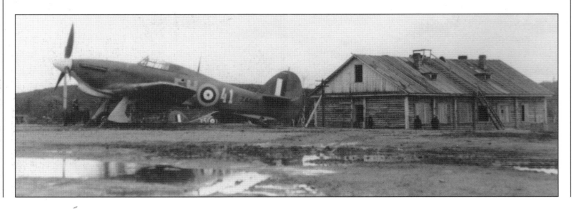

about 200 yards range, firing a three-second burst with no visible effect. The aircraft then turned to the right across me, and I delivered a quarter attack from about 150 yards, firing another burst of three seconds. During this attack smoke began to pour from the aircraft, a large piece flew off him and he rolled onto his back and went into a vertical dive. The pilot baled out.'

Soon afterwards Plt Off Bush shot down another Messerschmitt.

Defensive patrols then predominated, as no escorts were possible due to bad weather. By then No 151 Wing's other task – training Soviet pilots on the Hurricane – was well underway. Much of the instruction was done by Jack Ross, and one of the first pupils he sent solo was Capt Boris Safanov, who became a 16-victory ace. On 26 September, No 81 Sqn met more success when Flt Lt Mickey Rook and his wingman downed a Bf 109. The following day 12 Hurricanes escorted Pe 2s to Petsamo, where they were attacked by four Bf 109Es. In a turning fight Haw (in Z4018) hit one. It climbed, stalled, then dropped away pouring smoke. Haw's third kill over Russia made him No 151 Wing's top scorer, subsequently earning him the unique award of the Order of Lenin.

No 81 Sqn had seen the most action, but on 6 October it was No 134's turn at last when Vaenga was attacked by 14 Ju 88s from Banak. Two were brought down, four probably destroyed and five damaged. Flt Lt Mickey Rook, flying Z5207/FO, had been acting as weaver to one section and, becoming separated, flew towards what he thought were No 134's aircraft. He joined them, waggling his wings, only to discover that they were six Bf 109s of I./JG 77 – the Ju 88s' escort. In a furious dogfight he managed to destroy one of the fighters, reportedly blowing it to pieces, but was then chased at low level almost to Vaenga by the remainder. On landing, his black moustache bristling, Rook said 'the Germans must have thought me either bloody brave or bloody foolish'. His log book entry put it another way;

'Intercepted 14 Ju 88s. Helped damage one. Joined six '109s, damaged one, destroyed one. Dogfight with others, one bullet through my tail. CO, one Ju 88 destroyed.'

This was the RAF's last significant encounter with the Luftwaffe over Russia. On 18 October the aircraft were handed over to the Soviets, the Wing's score being 15 kills for the loss of just one Hurricane.

Two alumni of No 81 Sqn on the Russia expedition were Flt Sgt 'Wag' Haw (right) who, with three Bf 109s, was the top scorer, and his CO, Sqn Ldr Tony Rook (left). Both men were awarded the Order of Lenin by the Soviets. The pilot in the centre remains unidentified (*N L R Franks*)

No 134 Sqn's Hurricanes, including Z5236/GO-31 and Z5159/GV-33, taxi onto a snow-covered airfield at the start of another patrol over the Arctic frontline in early October 1941 (*P H T Green collection*)

MEDITERRANEAN BATTLES

At the start of 1941 the Luftwaffe began deploying its elite *Fleigerkorps* X to Sicily to support the Italians, as well as to secure the move of the *Afrika Korps* to Libya. Malta's first action of 1941 came on 9 January, and the following day *Fleigerkorps* X launched a furious air attack on the carrier HMS *Illustrious*. Heavily damaged, the vessel limped into Grand Harbour that night. The warship's presence signalled a series of further attacks as it underwent emergency repairs, thus beginning Malta's long torment. For the time being the defence largely rested in the hands of No 261 Sqn's Hurricanes.

On 18 January Flt Lt George Burges destroyed a Ju 87 to make himself an ace. The following day Flt Lt Maclachlan, in V7546, led the island's defenders straight into an enemy formation, shooting down two Stukas,

One of the veteran Hurricane Is of No 261 Sqn was P3731/J, which was flown regularly by Malta ace Sgt Fred Robertson, who claimed his sixth victory in it on 19 January 1941. Other aces who made claims flying this aircraft were Sgt Harry Ayre and Plt Off John Pain (*via R C B Ashworth*)

Sgt Fred Robertson is seen standing at the extreme left of this group of pilots at Ta Kali. He was the most successful Hurricane exponent in the Malta theatre. The pilot in the middle wearing sunglasses is Sgt C S Bamburger, who destroyed two Ju 87s over the island in January 1941 (*J Pickering*)

Having claimed seven victories, Flt Lt George Burges returned to reconnaissance duties with No 69 Sqn at Luqa. Modified into a PR platform on the island in order to cover more dangerous targets, Hurricane I V7109 was flown on a number of missions by Burges in May and June 1941 (*R H Barber*)

as did Burges. Malta veteran Sgt Fred Robertson also brought down a Ju 87 and a Fiat CR.42, thus becoming an ace. Awarded a DFM in March, by the time he was rested in April he had 11.5 victories to his name, making him the most successful Hurricane pilot over Malta. After refuelling Maclachlan took off again;

'At about 100 yards I opened fire. It was a huge three-engined job (a Cant Z506B of 612° *Squadriglia*, flown by S/Ten Rossi and crew – author). I could hardly have missed if I'd tried. A sheet of flame burst from its starboard wing root, so I ceased firing. It didn't seem to be losing height, but instead flew calmly on with flames and smoke pouring from it. I gave it another short squirt but it was already doomed.'

Maclachlan had now also become an ace.

The attacks eventually began to tail off, and *Illustrious* limped out to Egypt on the 23rd. Reinforcements arrived soon afterwards, including Plt Offs John Pain and Tony Rippon and Flt Lt Teddy Peacock-Edwards. They were soon in action, as Pain wrote;

'1 February saw my first blooding over Malta in a fight with Ju 88s and Me 109s, which started over the main island and finished off over Gozo, where I clobbered an '88.'

Things soon changed markedly for the worse with the appearance of the Bf 109Es of Oberleutnant Joachim Muncheberg's 7./JG 26, which shot down several Hurricanes, including Maclachlan's. He lost part of his left arm and was evacuated. During mid-March the hard-pressed No 261 Sqn was reinforced by a flight from No 274 Sqn, led by the formidable Flg Off 'Imshi' Mason.

The day they arrived, No 261 had engaged CR.42s from 23° *Gruppo* CT, which John Pain recalled

Plt Off Tony Rippon of No 261 Sqn was one of the most successful Hurricane pilots in Malta during the early months of 1941, being credited with at least four enemy aircraft destroyed and two shared between 5 March and 29 April (*B Cull*)

25

'…was the usual madhouse performance the Italians always seemed to put on – a real World War 1-style dogfight. I got my first in the sea close to Sliema'. This was his fifth success. On the 23rd Peacock-Edwards, Rippon and Sgt Harry Ayre also became aces. Flying V7430, Ayre shot down a Ju 87 to achieve his final victory.

——— REINFORCEMENTS ARRIVE ———

In early April reinforcements arrived aboard HMS *Ark Royal*, the new pilots including veterans Flt Lt 'Boy' Mould and Flg Off Innes Westmacott. Nevertheless, the marauding Bf 109s continued to exact a toll. 'Imshi' Mason described a scramble on 13 April;

'I came out of the sun into them and got my chap beautifully. He dived straight down. As I broke away from my attack, one of the other three got a lucky shot at me and hit my hand and shattered my windscreen.'

Mason ditched his aircraft, breaking his nose in the process, but he was soon picked up by a rescue boat, having become Oberleutnant Mietusch's eighth victim. On the 20th Flg Off Charles Laubscher and John Pain intercepted the first Italian raid on Grand Harbour for some time. Laubscher relates how he began his journey towards becoming an ace;

'I saw seven biplanes heading directly towards us in a shallow vic formation. We closed rapidly and I opened fire at about 800 yards, sighting a little high at first, then dropping my bead to centre on the machine. In two or three seconds we had passed directly over them. I immediately went into a steep turn to port to attack them again. I saw to my great satisfaction that the centre of the vic was empty.'

On 27 April further Hurricanes were flown off *Ark Royal*. As if to give the new arrivals a taste of what was to come, the enemy had laid on a strafing attack. One flight moved from Luqa to Hal Far, but the depredations continued. When the Balkans fell in May Malta was subjected to further assault. On the 4th Flt Lt 'Porky' Jefferies achieved his first Malta kill;

'I was "Yellow 1", patrolling ten miles east-north-east of Kalafrana at 29,500 ft, when I sighted a vapour trail I identified as a Ju 88. I made a quarter attack from above and to starboard, opening fire at 300 yards, closing to 50 yards. I finished my ammunition from astern. My port wing was covered in oil from the Ju 88.'

'C' Flight's victim was '4D+CT' of 9./KG 30 which crashed on its return to base.

In mid-May, with more pilots available, No 261's 'C' Flt became No 185 Sqn at Hal Far, the unit flying Hurricane IIBs under the leadership of 'Boy' Mould – No 261 Sqn was allowed to begin its withdrawal. The predatory Bf 109s continued to make life difficult, although No 261 had a rare success on the morning of the 15th, as John Pain recalled;

'I was scrambled after an early morning recce flight was detected. I chased him west along the south coast of the island. There was no doubt he crashed into the sea, as I watched him hit.'

The conditions the Hurricane squadrons endured on Malta are readily apparent as Hurricanes of No 249 Sqn burn at Ta Kali after being strafed by Bf 109s of Oberleutnant Muncheberg's 7./JG 26 on 25 May 1941 (*R Rist*)

It was the squadron's final victory over Malta, for within days a further reinforcement arrived at Takali (now Ta' Qali) in the shape of the experienced No 249 Sqn under Sqn Ldr 'Butch' Barton. At the same time, much of the Luftwaffe in Sicily was transferred to Russia.

Barton claimed his unit's first Malta victory on 1 June, as he noted in his log book – 'S.79 shot down into sea on fire off Gozo. No crew known to have escaped'. No 46 Sqn, under the charismatic ace Sqn Ldr Sandy Rabagliati, arrived too, having flown off the carriers *Ark Royal* and *Furious*. One of his pilots, Flg Off John Carpenter, recalled the flight specifically for this volume;

'No 46 Sqn flew off the carrier some 200 miles south of Sicily and flew at 500 ft all the way to Malta. It was not comfortable – we had 500-gal drop tanks, and all our kit was stuffed in empty spaces. We could only fly straight and level, anxious not to be seen or intercepted by enemy aircraft in this position. Thank goodness for the Merlin engine – not a cough or splutter, it ran like a sewing machine. Next day the air raids started, mainly the Italian Air Force, so we had a breathing space.'

Of his CO he said, 'Sqn Ldr "Rags" Rabagliati was one of the nicest and best COs a unit could ever have. He led us to Malta, and we were there for over a year.'

The newcomers' first action came on 11 June when they intercepted an SM.79. It was shot down by several pilots, including the CO. Early the following day Hurricanes fought a major engagement against some 30 Macchis. Leading the No 249 Sqn section was Flt Lt Tom Neil, who eloquently described his only victory over Malta;

'I fired. My tracer, with its familiar flicks of curving, whipping red, reached out and clutched both fuselage and wings in a brief rippling embrace.'

No 249 lost two Hurricanes, but No 46 Sqn caught the intruders. Flt Lt 'Pip' Lefevre fired at several Macchis, and reported that one crashed straight into the sea under his fire. It was his first claim over Malta and his fifth in total. It was No 46 (re-numbered No 126 Sqn on the 28th) which saw most of the action during the rest of June. Successful pilots included Sandy Rabagliati, while on the 30th 'Chips' Carpenter found a group of fighters and shot down a C.200;

'I chased one of them at sea level, only catching it when I pulled the emergency boost. I gave it a three-second burst at 250 yards. The Macchi didn't attempt to pull out of its dive and went straight into the sea.'

Hurricane IIB Z2961/K of No 185 Sqn was flown by a number of notable pilots over Malta, including Plt Off David Barnwell (five victories plus two shared), Sgt Tony Boyd (five plus two shared) and Sgt Garth Horricks (seven plus two shared). It shared in the destruction of a Ju 88 on 23 March 1942 (*P H P Roberts*)

No 185 Sqn's pilots pose for a group photo in July 1941. Seated in the centre, wearing a light shirt, is the CO, Sqn Ldr 'Boy' Mould, who was killed in action on 1 October, having taken his total score to 8.5 victories. On his immediate right is fellow ace Flt Lt 'Porky' Jeffries, who had a total of about four victories and two shared (*K Cox*)

One of the pilots who rose to prominence in Malta in the second half of 1941 was South African Plt Off Pat Lardner-Burke. On 6 November, after claiming his sixth Italian fighter destroyed, he was badly wounded and eventually evacuated to the UK (*B Cull*)

This was his fourth victory, but he had to wait until September for his fifth.

Day and night raids by the Italians continued through July, and it was during this time that 'Porky' Jeffries of No 185 Sqn became an ace. On the 11th Plt Off David Barnwell shot down his first victim in a short, but meteoric, career over Malta. On the 19th Sqn Ldr George Powell-Sheddan formed a new Hurricane unit at Takali, the Malta Night Fighter Unit (MNFU). Battle of France ace Flt Lt 'Dimsie' Stones was a flight commander. The unit's first success came on the night of 5/6 August when three Fiat BR.20Ms of 43° *Stormo* BT were shot down – David Barnwell got two of them. Two nights later it was the CO's turn to claim his only victory over Malta. He found a BR. 20 in the searchlights and made two attacks on it, but having lost his night vision, he failed to see *Tenente* Vercelli's MM22626 crash into the sea on fire.

THE ACES FALL

The next big engagement came on 4 September when six Italian fighters were claimed, including that of Spanish Civil War veteran *Ten Col* Romagnoli. One fell to John Carpenter, who thereby became an ace. The MNFU saw further action that night when, before dawn, Barnwell and Stones brought down a 9° *Stormo* Z1007bis.

Malta remained a constant thorn in the enemy's side, with its strike force interdicting supply lines across the Mediterranean. The Hurricane units then started flying fighter-bomber missions to Sicily, where they first encountered the new Macchi C.202 fighter, which appeared over Malta on 1 October. Sqn Ldr Mould, in Z5265/GL-T, fell to the elegant new Macchis of 9° *Gruppo* that very day, and they also claimed David Barnwell on the 14th. But there were some successes. On 8 November, in the biggest dogfight for some time, 18 C.200s and C.202s were engaged by a section from No 126 Sqn as they escorted bombers bound for

Malta. Plt Off Pat Lardner-Burke, in BD789/HA-G, shot down his fifth victim, but was immediately hit and wounded, although he managed to return.

The attacks on Sicily continued, and over Gela on the 12th, newly-arrived 19-victory ace Wg Cdr 'Hilly' Brown was shot down and killed by flak. That day, however, the Hurricanes of Nos 242 and 605 Sqns arrived at Hal Far to bring welcome reinforcement. At the same time the MNFU became No 1435 Flt, led by Sqn Ldr Innes Westmacott.

RETURN OF THE LUFTWAFFE

Ominously, however, Luftwaffe units again began returning to Sicily, and they made their first appearance on 19 December as a convoy approached Malta. A Ju 88 was claimed by eight-victory ace Sqn Ldr Stan Norris, No 126 Sqn's new CO. Later in the day three Ju 88 nightfighters on a day mission were intercepted, and No 249's new CO, Sqn Ldr Mortimer-Rose, who had nine victories from the UK, shot down 'R4+HH' to score his first victory over Malta. That afternoon, though, the Ju 88Cs were accompanied by JG 53's Bf 109Fs, and by the end of the month ten Hurricane pilots had been killed. Four died on 29 December alone.

One future alumni having his baptism of fire that day was Plt Off Sonny Ormrod of No 605 Sqn. He confided to his diary 'not too good for the Hurricane boys here, '109s having a much superior performance'. It was a tragically prophetic remark. The final claims of the year, on 30 December, also included a Ju 88 for Takali Wing Leader Wg Cdr Jack Satchell, the fourth of his seven victories.

Early on 3 January 1942 aircraft of Nos 126, 185 and 249 Sqns scrambled from Takali and a Ju 88 was shot down. It was credited to several pilots, including Sgt Garth Horricks, who was making his first claim. He was wounded in the arm and two Hurricanes were lost. Weather then restricted operations somewhat, although attacks came whenever conditions were suitable. A typical day was 8 February, after breakfast, Sqn Ldr Norris led a scramble. He was hit by return fire from a Ju 88 and crash-landed at Luqa with his engine on fire.

The rate of attrition was so bad that all airworthy fighters had to be consolidated into one unit, with squadrons at Takali or Hal Far flying them on alternate days. On the 12th Plt Off Oliver 'Sonny' Ormrod of No 605 Sqn was scrambled in cannon-armed Mk IIC BE351/LE-Y (notionally of No 242 Sqn). The section attacked a Ju 88 and shared in its demise. The bomber was Ormrod's first success, as he wrote in his diary;

'The other Hurricanes had already done damage and I saw the port engine was smoking. Saw one of the crew bale out as I opened fire at 150 yards. Immediately flames shot up from the starboard engine. Oil smothered my aircraft as I pulled hard on the stick to avoid colliding with

Hurricane IIC BE402/LE-S was one of the aircraft ferried to Malta with No 242 Sqn in late 1941, and it is seen here after a taxying mishap on Christmas Day. In the desperate circumstances of early 1942, aircraft were flown by any available pilots, and Sqn Ldr Innes Westmacott of No 1435 Flt used this machine to share in the probable destruction of a Ju 88 on the night of 7/8 March (*C F Shores*)

the enemy. I skimmed just over the top of him, knowing that I had delivered the *coup de grace*.'

The bombers inflicted further damage in what were now daily raids. More pilots continued to arrive on the island by flying boat, including the redoubtable Sqn Ldr Stan Turner who took over No 249 Sqn. The unit subsequently re-equipped with Spitfires, deliveries of which also allowed other units to retire their Hurricanes over the next couple of months.

Intense action continued, and Australian Sgt John Boyd opened his account on 23 February when he shot down Bf 109 'White 4' of 10./JG53. He wrote, 'got into position and fired four-second burst from astern. Obviously got him'. A few days later the youthful Ormrod, having escaped the Bf 109 escort, bagged another Ju 88 over Grand Harbour;

'I took a shot from a quarter astern at about 300 yards, then held my fire until I was about 200 yards astern. I fired. Smoke began emerging from both engines. The aircraft was then losing height in a shallow dive.'

Ormrod's first 'solo' victory was witnessed by many on the ground.

February closed with the pilots of Nos 242 and 605 Sqns being absorbed into Nos 126 and 185 Sqns respectively. The bad situation for the depleted Hurricane units was to get immeasurably worse. Malta's battering continued unabated into March. with the defenders taking increasing losses. Another concentrated raid on Takali was followed by a strafing attack by Bf 110s of III./ZG 26. These were in turn engaged by Plt Offs Sonny Ormrod and Wigley, now of No 185 Sqn. They shared in the destruction of one of the Bf 110s – apparently '3U+FT' – to bring Ormrod his fifth success.

On 25 February dive-bombers attacked a convoy newly arrived in port, and a Ju 87 fell to Sgt Garth Horricks, giving him ace status. The next day No 126 Sqn's new 'boss', Sqn Ldr 'Jumbo' Gracie, entered combat. Soon afterwards further reinforcements flew in when ten Hurricane IICs of No 229 Sqn's 'A' Flight arrived from Egypt. Almost immediately they came under the leadership of Flt Lt Paul Farnes, an ace from 1940.

Although Spitfires shouldered more of the load, one Hurricane pilot who continued to claim consistently was John Boyd of No 185 Sqn, and he was awarded a DFM in April, as was Horricks. Sonny Ormrod received a DFC, but as the fighting took a steady toll, he was lost on 22 April chasing a Ju 88 over Grand Harbour. He was to be the final ace killed in a Hurricane in action over Malta.

There was a brief respite from the torment in the middle of April, during which the remainder of No 229 Sqn arrived under eight-victory ace Flt Lt Bob Dafforn, who was promoted to CO on arrival. Wounded soon afterwards, he was replaced by Farnes. By May the Hurricane's time over Malta had almost come to an end, although on the 7th Flt Sgt Gordon Tweedale, an aggressive young Australian, claimed his fifth victory. The following day saw the final Hurricane victories over Malta, scored appropriately

Hurricane IIA BV163/HA-F wears the codes of No 126 Sqn, although it was being used by No 185 Sqn in March 1942. The Australian ace Flt Sgt Gordon Tweedale flew it when he damaged a Bf 109 on 4 April, and he also used it to claim his final victories – a Ju 88 and a Bf 109F (and a second Bf 109 as a probable) of 8./JG 53 on 8 May. Twelve days prior to this the fighter had been damaged in a crash-landing by No 229's CO, Sqn Ldr Bob Dafforn, who had been wounded in combat (*D H Newton*)

Surviving members of No 229 Sqn pose at Hal Far just before departing for Egypt on 27 May 1942. On the wing, from left to right, are Flt Sgt R L K Carson and Plt Offs K L Lee and D J Carter, whilst in the front row, left to right, are Sgts N A Ganes, Alderdice and R V Potts, Sqn Ldr P C P Farnes DFM (CO), Flt Sgt D Roy, Sgts G H Willcox, N L Vidler and J B Pauley and Plt Off L G Malthus. On detachment from their parent unit, these men had flown in ten reinforcement Hurricane IICs on 27 March, but had only claimed one probable Ju 87 and several damaged for the loss of six pilots killed and five aircraft shot down. A further 15 Hurricanes were lost to enemy air attacks or accidents (*T E Lawrence*)

by two of the more successful pilots of recent weeks. Tweedale, in BV163/HA-F, and Boyd, flying Z4942/GL-Y, scrambled, and the subsequent action was eloquently described in the squadron diary;

'"Tweedle" went to town with a vengeance and proceeded to shoot up everything in the sky, with the result that one Ju 88 and one Me 109 "went for a burton."'

Boyd was credited with a Ju 88.

The following day 64 Spitfires left the decks of HMS *Eagle* and USS *Wasp* and were immediately handed over to the experienced Malta pilots. This proved a tragic decision, as that evening, on his first sortie, Gordon Tweedale was shot down and killed. Boyd fell on the 14th. The Spitfires were now in the ascendant, and on 27 May the battered survivors of No 229 Sqn left for Egypt.

CARRIER ACTION

Sustaining Malta was now a major priority for the Royal Navy. During the vital convoy battles of mid-1942 the Sea Hurricane entered the fray aboard the carrier HMS *Eagle*, 813 NAS's fighter flight of four and 801 NAS (led by Lt Cdr Rupert Brabner, the sitting MP for Hythe) being in the vanguard. In June the carrier participated in Operation *Harpoon* to fight a convoy through to Malta from Gibraltar. It was soon under aerial surveillance. In the early evening of 13 June Lt King-Joyce, whose aircraft became unserviceable soon after launching, and Sub Lt Crosley of 813 NAS were launched. Crosley said;

'As I strained my eyes, willing myself to see something, the unbelievable happened. I could see a black spot moving slowly eastwards, about five miles to the south. I immediately called "Bogey, three o'clock below, five miles, turning now, over". As the range decreased, I could clearly see that it was a three-engined aircraft with exhaust smoke coming from the engines. It was now a chase. I knew I would win, and came up from below and astern, thus keeping clear of his slipstream. I had overtaking speed of at least 40 knots and had to push the stick forward quickly before I got in too close and within range of his four rear guns. I was breathing hard.

'With cloud cover only a short distance ahead, I pulled back on the stick, got his underside flying into the centre of the ring-sight and pressed the firing button. As I did so, I could see sparks coming from the Cant's tail. Then I could see smoke coming from the port side. I continued firing through the smoke. I overshot him as I turned away into the clear, and could see that his port wing and engine had flames coming from them, as well as smoke. He was already turning slowly to port and losing height. When his aircraft touched the sea it left a trail of yellow pieces of fuselage behind in its wake.'

He had shot down the aircraft of *Ten* Piccioni of 212° *Squadriglia*, this being the first of his 4.5 victories.

The following morning, Mike Crosley attacked Unteroffizier Schwarz's Ju 88D 'F6+EH' of 1(F)./122, which was later confirmed as shot down. Later he claimed an SM.79 as a probable. 801 NAS was also busy, and the CO destroyed a C.200 and an SM.79. He also shared a reconnaissance Ju 88 with Sub Lt Peter Hutton, who also shot down a Junkers bomber by himself. That night, after a day of heavy fighting, the carriers and their heavy escort turned back west of the Sicilian Narrows.

In spite of this convoy, Malta was soon once again in desperate straits, and in August another fast convoy was planned. It was to be the epic convoy known as Operation *Pedestal*. The escort included four carriers, three of which were equipped with Sea Hurricanes – *Eagle* with 801 and 813 NASs, *Victorious* with Lt R H P Carver's new 885 NAS and *Indomitable* with 800 and 880 NASs. These units comprised some of the Navy's most experienced fighter pilots, with Lt Cdr 'Bill' Bruen CO of 800 NAS and Lt W H Martyn its senior pilot, while 880 NAS's CO was Lt Dickie Cork.

The operation got under way on 10 August, with the action beginning early on the 11th. The first major casualty was HMS *Eagle*, which was torpedoed and sunk that afternoon, taking all but four of its Hurricanes to the bottom. Those airborne at the time of the attack landed on *Victorious* and *Indomitable*. The air battle reached a crescendo on the 12th, with a number of notable pilots playing a leading role. Lt Cdr Bruen, in Z4550/G, launched on an early patrol and destroyed a Ju 88 for his fifth kill, and at noon he shared in the destruction of an SM.84. Later during the sortie he downed an SM.79, which crashed into the sea.

Another to become an ace was Lt William 'Moose' Martyn, who, just after 0900 hrs, led his section into a formation of Ju 88s at 18,000 ft. He immediately shot one down and hit the starboard engine of a second, which was finished off by his wingman. Later, when south of Sardinia, Sub Lt Blythe Ritchie of 800 NAS downed two Ju 87Ds (probably 'S7+HL' and 'CG+SK' of I./StG 3),

The aircraft in the foreground is Sea Hurricane IB Z4550/G of 800 NAS, and it is seen here just minutes before taking off from the deck of HMS *Indomitable* during the epic Operation *Pedestal* convoy to Malta. Lt Cdr Bill Bruen was flying this machine on 12 August 1942 when he became an ace, initially destroying a Ju 88 and, on a later sortie, an SM.79. He also shared in the destruction of an SM.84 on this day (*N Robinson*)

and shared a third. These were his first claims, although he became an ace flying Hellcats in 1944.

801 NAS's survivors on *Victorious* also saw action, Brabner hitting an SM.79 and an SM.84, which were initially considered to be probables. Both were later upgraded to destroyed, making Brabner an ace, which was probably a unique distinction for a sitting MP. Another migrant was Sub Lt Hutton, who shot down an Re.2001 and later a Loire 70 flying boat, taking him to 3.5 destroyed. Most successful

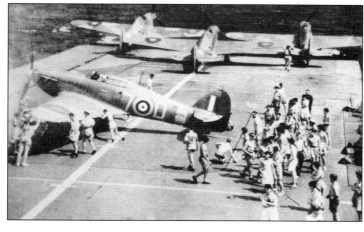

Sea Hurricane IB AF974/7-D of 880 NAS is repositioned on the flightdeck of HMS *Indomitable*. During Operation *Pedestal* this aircraft probably destroyed a Ju 88 over the fleet when flown by Sub Lt Brownlee (*author's collection*)

during the day, however, was Dickie Cork of 880 NAS. He shot down an SM.79 over the convoy at 1230 hrs and then destroyed a Ju 88 off the Tunisian coast and shared in the destruction of another. Later, Cork also shot down a Bf 110 and another SM.79 to become the only Royal Navy pilot to claim five enemy aircraft destroyed in a day, for which he was awarded the DSO. He was held in high esteem, as a colleague explained. 'He had the quality men follow. An immaculate pilot, he moved with the radiance of a head prefect, taking the worship of the lesser fry for granted.'

That evening, as the heavy escort prepared to withdraw, *Indomitable* was hit and badly damaged. But the epic *Pedestal* battle had also signalled the end of the Hurricane's part in the Malta saga.

A GREEK TRAGEDY

On 28 October 1940 Italian forces invaded Greece, and among the RAF units despatched was the experienced Gladiator-equipped No 80 Sqn. It would soon make its mark. In mid February 1941 No 80 received some Hurricanes, which arrived for operations at Paramythia, near the Albanian border. At the same time No 33 Sqn's Hurricanes moved to Greece from North Africa, the unit numbering among its ranks several

Two of No 80 Sqn's most notable pilots in Greece were Sgt Ted Hewett, left, and next to him, Plt Off Bill Vale. Third from the right is the greatest of them all, Flt Lt Pat Pattle (*J McGaw*)

This Hurricane I of No 33 Sqn at Paramythia in March 1941 appears to be V7804. It was flown in the battle over Athens on 20 April by Flt Lt Harry Starrett when he shared in the destruction of two Ju 88s, but was hit by return fire. Starrett suffered burns so severe that he died two days later (*E L Cooper*)

successful pilots such as Flg Offs Charles Dyson (nine victories), Vernon Woodward (eight), Frank Holman (one), Peter Wickham (four) and John Mackie (six), and Flt Sgt Len Cottingham (six).

No 80 Sqn flew the first Hurricane operation in Greece on the 20th, led by the unit's leading pilot, Flt Lt 'Pat' Pattle. On the way back Pattle spotted some Italian fighters, as his biography relates;

'He led his section straight towards four Fiat G.50s and, shouting to Sgt Casbolt and "Timber" Woods to attack individually, selected the leading G.50 as his own target. As he approached, the dark green Fiat pulled away into a steep turn, but Pat managed to hold it in his sights until he came into range and thumbed the gun button. It was the first time he had fired the eight guns of the Hurricane, and the result was astonishing. The G.50 exploded right before his eyes, disintegrating into hundreds of small flaming pieces.'

The Hurricane had shot down its first victim over Greece. Casbolt claimed two, and after landing, so did Woods. It was a highly successful debut which ensured that the RAF's moral ascendancy was maintained. Pattle's Fiat was from 154° *Gruppo*, and it was the first of around 35 victories that the South African would claim while flying the Hurricane over the next two months.

No 33's detachment began operations alongside No 80 Sqn on 27 February when it intercepted Italian bombers (escorted by CR.42s) over Valona. The unit's Sgt Ted Hewett claimed two to take his total to five, while No 33's Sgt Len Cottingham scored his outfit's first Hurricane victory, which also made him and ace, and Flg Off Harry Starrett shared another. The next afternoon there was a huge dogfight between RAF and Italian fighters over the frontline. The Italians were routed, although British claims for 27 destroyed were certainly inflated. Pattle, in V7589, destroyed two fighters and two Fiat BR.20 bombers of 37° *Stormo*. Flg Off Richard Acworth (detached from No 112 Sqn) also sent down a BR.20 for his fifth. Flg Off 'Ape' Cullen (who had flown V7138) wrote of his first Hurricane combat;

'The battle extended right across Albania. First, I found four Breda 20s (sic). I got one, which went down in flames Then we found three formations of SM.79s. I took on one and aimed at the starboard engine. It caught fire and crashed in flames. I climbed and dived on the next. He too crashed in flames. Then we attacked ten CR.42s, climbing to get above them. I got behind one, and he caught fire and went down in flames. Up again immediately – dived, fired into the cockpit and another took fire, rolled over and crashed. I had to come home then – no more ammo.'

After this extraordinary combat the young Australian received an immediate DFC. Meanwhile, Pattle had landed and then returned to the fray in another aircraft and shot down two more CR.42s. It was the RAF's most successful day of the campaign.

During the morning of 3 March Cullen, Acworth and Plt Off Bill Vale intercepted a mixed formation of Z1007 and SM.81 bombers heading for Larissa. Acworth shot down one Cant, Cullen claimed four more and Vale scored his first Hurricane kill (his 14th victory), recording tersely in his log book, '1025, interception Patrol (one S.81)'. The next day both squadrons escorted a force attacking Italian warships. As they neared Valona six G.50s dived on them, Pattle sending one into a mountainside north of Himare. However, a second Fiat jumped Cullen and the 15-victory Australian ace crashed and was killed. Pattle continued, shooting down two more G.50s, while Sgt Hewett was also busy claiming a G.50 and three CR.42s. Bill Vale also shot down a G.50.

Pattle left the squadron shortly afterwards to take command of No 33 Sqn. He was regarded with the utmost respect by his peers, one of whom, Sqn Ldr (later Air Marshal Sir) Paddy Dunn said of him that 'air fighting was his game. Pattle was a remarkable man, with an easy and natural manner. In Greece his courage and indomitable leadership became legendary – an exceptional fighter leader and a brilliant pilot'.

On 23 March Sqn Ldr Pattle led an attack against Fier airfield, where they were jumped by 20 G.50s. One fell to 'Woody' Woodward, another to Pattle and the third to fellow No 33 Sqn 'aces, Flg Off Frank Holman. At around this time, during a lull in the fighting, No 80 Sqn at last became fully re-equipped with Hurricanes. There were some Italian attacks during this period, such as on 2 April when a group of Z1007s lost three of their number to 'Woody' Woodward. He shot two down in flames on his first diving pass before attacking a third, which ditched in the Gulf of Patras.

BLITZKRIEG!

On 6 April the Germans invaded the Balkans, and at a stroke they transformed the situation in Greece for the British. The RAF was soon in action and, as ever, Pattle was to the fore when No 33 Sqn mounted an offensive patrol over Bulgaria. There, he claimed his first German victims – Bf 109Es from 8./JG 27. Oberleutnant Arno Becker was killed and Leutnant Klaus Faber captured. Len Cottingham shot down a third Bf 109 and another fell to Flg Off Peter Wickham, his first success in the

Hurricane I V7419 (coded NW, but without an individual letter) acts as a backdrop to pilots of No 33 Sqn at Larissa in early April 1941. Standing, from left to right, are Plt Offs D S F Winsland, R Dunscombe and C A C Cheetham, and Flg Offs P R W Wickham (ten victories), D T Moir and H J Starrett (three victories plus four shared). Sitting, left to right, are Flg Offs E J Woods and F S Holman (8.5 victories), Flt Lt A M Young, Flg Off V C Woodward (18 victories plus four shared), Sqn Ldr M T StJ Pattle (50 plus two shared), Flg Off E H Dean (five), Flt Lts J M Littler and Flt Lt G Rumsey and Plt Off A R Butcher (*No 33 Sqn Records*)

Hurricane. However, the Greek collapse in eastern Macedonia allowed a rapid German move southwards, forcing a British withdrawal.

During the afternoon of 12 April Pattle led a sweep up the rugged Struma valley, where they encountered a lone Dornier which he shot down. Then directed to Larissa, his formation duly found three escorted SM.79s. Ordering some of his force to attack the fighters, Pattle led Harry Starret and Frankie Holman down on the bombers, claiming one while the other two shared a second. No 80 Sqn was also heavily engaged. During a bomber escort over Bulgaria on the 14th, Vale, in V7795, shot down a Ju 87, recording the event in his log book, '1250 – Bomber escort over Bulgaria (one Ju 87)'. This aircraft was probably the most successful individual Hurricane of the Greek campaign. Having been delivered to No 80 Sqn as a reinforcement on 9 April, it was regularly flown by Bill Vale over the next six weeks.

The Germans had begun heavy attacks on RAF airfields, and at Larissa on the 15th a future ace had a narrow escape. One of the groundcrew, AC 2 D F Harris described it vividly;

'I dashed out of our ridge tent to see a sight I'll never forget as three very brave pilots stood their Hurricanes on their tails to gain height – 15 yellow-nosed Messerschmitt 109s were coming at them out of the dawn sun. The first to go was Plt Off Chatham when his aircraft was cut in half by enemy fire. Flt Lt Jackie stalled in on one wing, his guns firing to the last. Sgt Genders gained some height and managed to survive to land later on. One of the '109s was shot down and the pilot baled out.'

AC Harris saw Jackie's victim fall. In his first combat George Genders brought down Feldwebel Kohler of 4./JG 77, and within a week the 21-year-old was credited with four more victories.

Another claiming his first victory that day was Plt Off Roald Dahl, who shot down a Ju 88, while Vale went one better by downing two Junkers bombers over Athens in V7795, getting another on the 16th and two Stukas over Larissa on the 18th.

DEATH OVER PIRAEUS

On 19 April – a day of continuous raids – Woodward shared Hs 126 '6K+AH' of 1(H)./23 with Pattle and another pilot. He recalled, 'Pattle was mad. He had gone down to attack the Hs 126 and the rest of the flight followed to join in the fun. No one thought to provide top cover'. Leaving the area, they met nine Bf 109s, but Pattle and Woodward pulled into Zimmerman turns that put them onto the tails of the enemy fighters, with the result that Sqn Ldr Pattle shot down two and Woodward one.

By now both Hurricane squadrons were greatly reduced in strength, and concentrated at Eleusis, near Athens. There they faced a sustained Luftwaffe assault. During an early patrol on the 20th, Frankie Holman belly-landed on marshy ground, but the aircraft overturned and the pilot broke his neck, killing him instantly. Worse was to follow that afternoon

Hurricane I V7795 is pictured while on a ferry flight to Greece on 9 April 1941, Battle of Britain ace Sgt Jock Norwell being at the controls. Passed to No 80 Sqn, it was used on the 14th by Plt Off Bill Vale to destroy a Ju 87 over Bulgaria, followed by two Ju 88s 24 hours later. After evacuating to Crete, Vale claimed five more victories in this aircraft, but what was probably the highest-scoring Hurricane of the ill-fated Greek campaign was destroyed at Maleme on 18 May (*J Pickering*)

Sgt George Eric Genders of No 33 Sqn made his first claim during an enemy strafing attack on Larissa which saw the two other Hurricane pilots who scrambled with him shot down. He scored a number of kills, notably three Ju 87s over Piraeus on 23 April, before being evacuated from Crete. Genders became a test pilot post-war, and was killed in the crash of the DH 108 Swallow on 1 May 1950 (*No 33 Sqn records*)

This Hurricane I, coded YK-L, bears mute testimony to the effectiveness of the Luftwaffe attacks at Eleusis. It was probably one of the survivors of the battle over Piraeus on 20 April (*via C H Goss*)

One pilot who enjoyed his first success during the desperate days of mid-April 1941 was Plt Off Roald Dahl, who claimed three Ju 88s before the evacuation from Greece (*author's collection*)

when a huge raid of over a hundred bombers, with fighter escort, was reported heading for the harbour at Piraeus to attack the shipping there. The last surviving Hurricanes – nine from No 33 and six from No 80 – were scrambled. Among the first to arrive over the port were Peter Wickham, Harry Starrett and Flg Off 'Ping' Newton. They followed some Ju 88s into their dives, Newton shooting down two for his first victories. Wickham also got another, while Bill Vale, who arrived to claim two, recalled, 'One caught fire and started going down so I left him and attacked another. Big chunks broke away from his wings and fuselage and smoke poured from his engines. He went down vertically'. Starrett, in V7804, was hit and caught fire. In an attempt to save his aircraft he headed for Eleusis, but as he touched down the Hurricane was enveloped in flames and he later succumbed to his injuries.

Other Hurricanes from No 80 Sqn were by now engaging the mass of Do 17s and Bf 110s. Sgt Casbolt claimed two, and as he pulled away a Bf 109 crossed his path and he sent it down in flames too. Sgt Ted Hewett attacked six Bf 109s, reporting, 'I dived on the rear one and he rolled on his back and crashed to the ground with smoke pouring out. I made a similar attack on a second and the pilot baled out'. These victories took his total to 16. Some pilots had retuned to Eleusis, and having replenished their fuel and ammunition, headed back to the fight led by a very sick Pattle on his third sortie of the day. Vernon Woodward later recalled;

'I took off late with Sqn Ldr Pattle. We climbed into a swarm of Ju 88s protected by masses of Messerschmitt 110s. We were overwhelmed. In sun, I recall shooting a '110 off Pattle's tail, in flames, then probably a Ju 88. Shortly afterwards Pattle got a confirmed '110. Subsequently, I lost contact with him.'

Ahead of him, Woodward had witnessed his CO attempting to aid his friend, 'Timber' Woods, who was being attacked by a Bf 110. He had seen its demise just as Woods' aircraft burst into flames and crashed into the bay. Two other Bf 110s then swept onto Pattle's Hurricane, which caught fire and exploded. It too crashed into Eleusis Bay, taking with it the RAF's most successful fighter pilot. His end was witnessed by Flt Lt Jimmie Kettlewell, who attacked and shot down one of the Bf 110s to score his fifth victory. Then he too was hit and forced to bale out, injuring his back on landing. Another of No 33's aces, Flt Sgt Len Cottingham, also baled out wounded, but not before he had downed three Bf 110s. It had been a truly disastrous afternoon for the RAF fighters.

CRETE

As British forces evacuated Greece, the remnants of No 33 Sqn flew to Maleme, on Crete, while most of No 80 Sqn went to Egypt. On 24 April Vale flew V7795 to Crete, having his first combat on 29 April when he shot down two Ju 88s.

The last Hurricane – W9298/X of No 33 Sqn was the final surviving fighter on Crete when the island was evacuated on 19 May 1941. On the 14th it had been flown by the squadron's new CO, Sqn Ldr E A Howell, when he made his first claims (one Bf 109 destroyed and a second damaged) off Maleme (*E A Howell*)

Crete proved to be a poor place to make a defensive stand, for there was little infrastructure on the airfields and attrition was steady. On 11 May many of No 33 Sqn's pilots were replaced, with Sqn Ldr E A Howell arriving to take command despite having never flown a Hurricane before! Vale, however, continued in action, shooting down a Ju 52/3m on the 13th. The first serious attack developed the following day when Ju 88s bombed Suda Bay and Maleme. Two Hurricanes scrambled. Sqn Ldr Howell (in W9298/X) was low over the sea when he spotted Bf 109s. 'I went right on the tail of the second '109 till I was in close formation on him. The Hurricane shook and shuddered as rounds poured into him, bits broke away and a white trail burst from his radiator as coolant came pouring out'. His first victory was probably Unteroffizier Hagel of 4./JG77.

On the 16th Bill Vale recorded the final kills of the campaign in his laconic style in his log book. '0615: raid alarm (one Me 109)'. Of his third sortie of the day he wrote, '1715: patrol Suda Bay (one Ju 87)'. Sqn Ldr Howell had also been successful, downing a Ju 52/3m while on a reconnaissance. It was the second of his eventual four kills. The writing was firmly on the wall, however, for the following day only one serviceable Hurricane remained, and it left for Egypt on the 19th. The next day the airborne invasion of Crete began, and Imperial forces again faced evacuation. Among others, No 274 Sqn's Hurricanes attempted to support Crete from North Africa. A contemporary account described Flt Lt Owen Tracey's elevation to ace status;

'Over Crete, Flt Lt Tracey, a 24-year-old New Zealander, disposed of an Me 109 in unique fashion. The '109 had fastened onto the tail of Tracey's Hurricane, so he power-dived towards the steep cliffs that formed the coastline of the island, pulled his aircraft clear at the last split second and left the '109 to dive to destruction. After bagging the '109, and a Ju 52, Tracey turned his badly riddled aircraft for home. In spite of having an aileron shot away, a cannon shell through the prop, one through a long range fuel tank and one through the tail wheel, which had torn along the fuselage, smashed the radio and dented the back of his armour plated seat, he managed to bring the Hurricane across 200 miles of open sea.'

In spite of such gallantry and determination, there was little that could be done. Crete soon fell, leaving the Axis powers firmly in control of the northern Mediterranean shores.

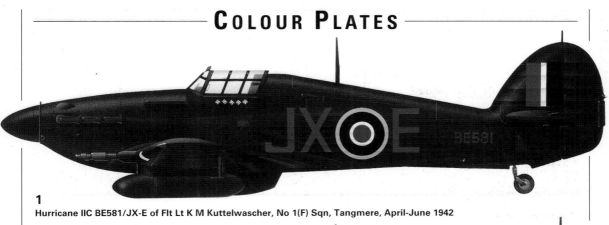

1
Hurricane IIC BE581/JX-E of Flt Lt K M Kuttelwascher, No 1(F) Sqn, Tangmere, April-June 1942

2
Hurricane IIB BE171/YB-B of Sgt J F Barrick, Mingaladon, No 17 Sqn, Burma, February 1942

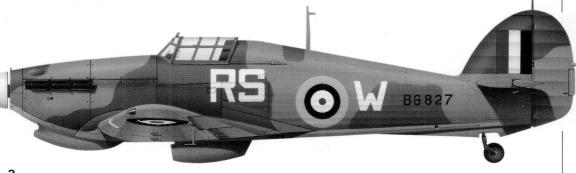

3
Hurricane IIB BG827/RS-W of Plt Off J H Whalen, No 30 Sqn, Ratmalana, Ceylon, April 1942

4
Hurricane IIC BP588/RS-X of Sqn Ldr S C Norris, No 33 Sqn, Benina, Libya, November-December 1942

5
Hurricane IIC BN230/FT-A of Sqn Ldr D A R G L Du Vivier, No 43 Sqn, Acklington, 25 April 1942

6
Hurricane I V7101 of Flt Lt G Burges, No 69 Sqn, Luqa, Malta, May 1941

7
Hurricane IIB Z3781/XR-T of Plt Off W R Dunn, No 71 'Eagle' Sqn, North Weald, July 1941

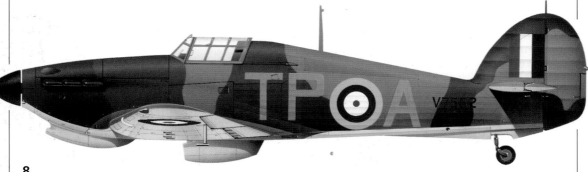

8
Hurricane I V7562/TP-A of Sgt A E Marshall, No 73 Sqn, Sidi Haneish, Egypt, 5 January 1941

9
Hurricane IIB Z3745/NV-B of Sqn Ldr G D L Haysom, No 79 Sqn, Fairwood Common, August 1941

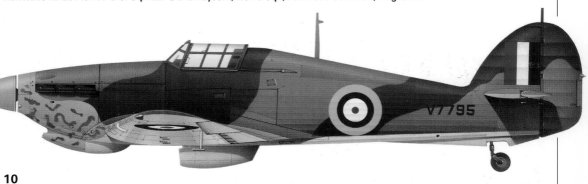

10
Hurricane I V7795 of Plt Off W Vale, No 80 Sqn, Eleusis, Greece, and Maleme, Crete, April-May 1941

11
Hurricane IIB Z4018/FH-41 of Flt Sgt C Haw, No 81 Sqn, Vaenga, Russia, September 1941

12
Hurricane I P3149/LK-P of Plt Off I J Badger, No 87 Sqn, St Mary's, Isles of Scilly, June-July 1941

13
Hurricane IIB Z3427/AV-R of Plt Off S R Edner, No 121 'Eagle' Sqn, Kirton-in-Lindsay, 8 August 1941

14
Hurricane IIB BD776/WG-F of Sqn Ldr J I Kilmartin, No 128 Sqn, Hastings, Sierra Leone, 3 April 1942

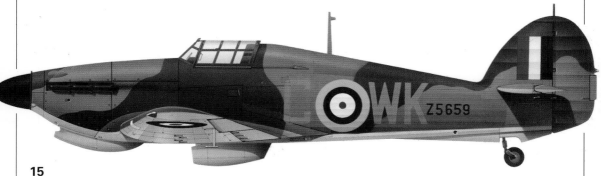

15
Hurricane IIB Z5659/WK-C of Plt Off W J Storey, No 135 Sqn, Mingaladon, Burma, February 1942

16
Hurricane IIB AP894/C of Flt Lt W J Storey, No 135 Sqn, 'George' and 'Hove' LGs, East Bengal, March-May 1943

17
Hurricane IIB BE198/HM-R of Plt Off A G Conway, No 136 Sqn, Red Road, Calcutta, India, 10 July 1942

18
Hurricane IIB BM913/N of Flt Lt E Brown, No 136 Sqn, Chittagong, East Bengal, May 1943

19
Hurricane I V6931/DZ-D of Flt Lt I S Smith, No 151 Sqn, Wittering, 10 May 1941

20
Hurricane IIB Z2961/K of Sgt G E Horricks, No 185 Sqn, Takali, Malta, 23 March 1942

21
Hurricane I Z4223/V of Flg Off G H Westlake, No 213 Sqn, Nicosia, Cyprus, July-October 1941

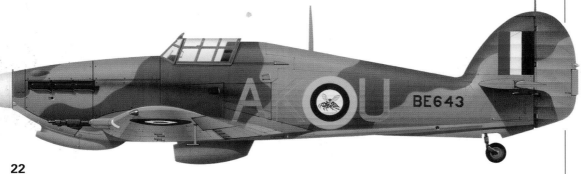

22
Hurricane IIC BE643/AK-U of Plt Off A U Houle, No 213 Sqn, Edku, Egypt, April 1942

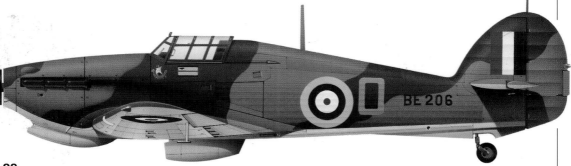

23
Hurricane IIB BE206/O of Flt Lt E W Wright, No 232 Sqn, Kallang, Singapore, 5 February 1942

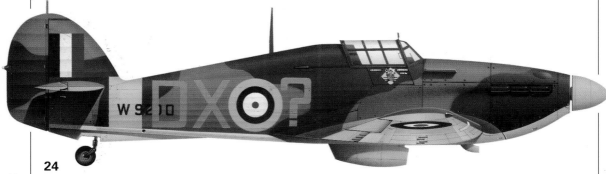

24
Hurricane I W9200/DX-? of Sqn Ldr J W C Simpson, No 245 Sqn, Aldergrove, Northern Ireland, 6 May 1941

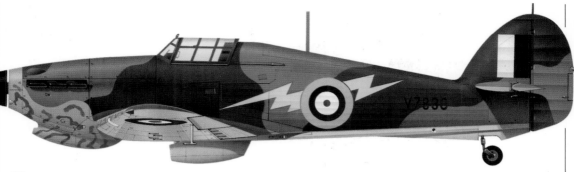

25
Hurricane I V7830 of Flg Off O V Tracey, No 274 Sqn, Gerawla, Egypt, 29 May 1941

26
Hurricane IIA DG631/NH-C of Flg Off W A G Conrad, No 274 Sqn, El Adem, Libya, 12 February 1942

27
Hurricane IIB Z3437/DU-K of Sgt O Kucera, No 312 'Czech' Sqn, Kenley, July 1941

28
Hurricane I V7339/JH-X of Sgt S Brzeski, No 317 'Wilenski' Sqn, Fairwood Common, 10 July 1941

29
Hurricane IIB BD734/FN-D of Sgt S Heglund, No 331 'Norwegian' Sqn, Skeabrae, Orkney, October-November 1941

30
Hurricane IIB BD707/AE-C of Flt Sgt G D Robertson, No 402 Squadron RCAF, Southend, 18 September 1941

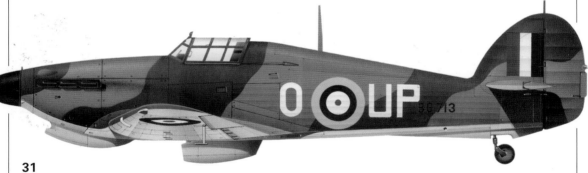

31
Hurricane IIB BG713/UP-O of Plt Off O Ormrod, No 605 Sqn, Hal Far, Malta, December 1941-January 1942

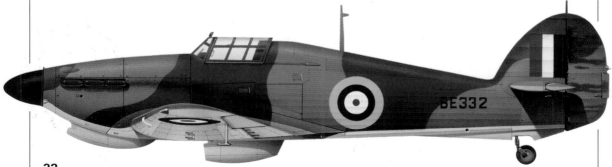

32
Hurricane IIB BE332 of Plt Off J A Campbell, No 605 Sqn, Tjililitan, Java, 25 February 1942

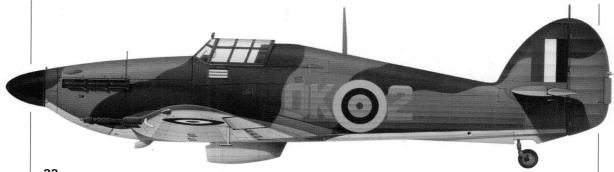

33
Hurricane IIC Z3574(?)/OK-2, personal aircraft of the AOC Malta, Air Vice Marshal K R Park, Luqa, Malta,
October-November 1942

34
Sea Hurricane IA V6802/LU-B of Plt Off A S C Lumsden, Merchant Ship Fighter Unit, MV *Daghestan*, North Atlantic,
September-October 1941

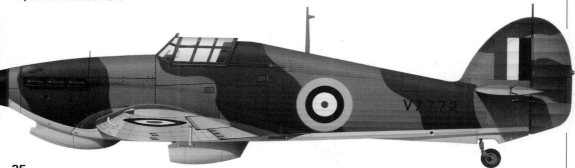

35
Hurricane I V7772 of Flg Off A C Rawlinson, No 3 Sqn RAAF, Amriya, Egypt, February 1941

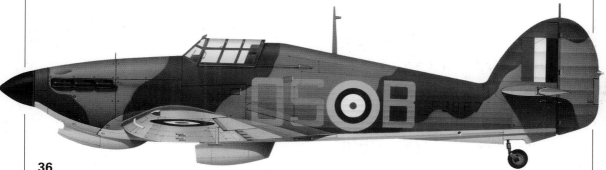

36
Hurricane I P3967/OS-B of Flt Lt J R Perrin, No 3 Sqn RAAF, Mararua, Libya, 5 April 1941

37
Hurricane IIB BG971/AX-V of Maj G J Le Mesurier, No 1 Sqn SAAF, LG 92, Egypt, 3 July 1942

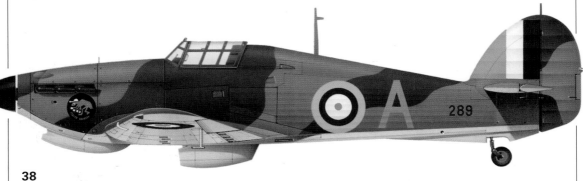

38
Hurricane I 289/A of Capt J E Frost, No 3 Sqn SAAF, Jigigga, Abyssinia, March-April 1941

39
Sea Hurricane IB Z4550/G of Lt Cdr J M Bruen, 800 NAS, HMS *Indomitable*, Malta convoy, 12 August 1942

40
Sea Hurricane IIB JS355 of Lt Cdr J M Bruen, 800 NAS, HMS *Biter*, Operation *Torch*, 8 November 1942

ABOVE THE DESERT

The beginning of 1941 saw British forces continuing their drive into Libya, during which time RAF fighter squadrons in the desert were able to maintain their ascendancy over the *Regia Aeronautica*. Hurricanes of Nos 33 and 274 Sqns flew patrols over the Gambut area and at mid-morning on 4 January, Sgt Tom Morris of the latter unit intercepted a formation of CR.42 biplanes, shooting one down to become an ace. He too had been hit, however, and he force-landed in the desert, returning to the squadron that evening.

The following day his CO, Sqn Ldr Paddy Dunn, led a fight against a formation of SM.79s, with CR.42 escort, south of Gambut, and he claimed a Fiat fighter for his ninth, and final, victory. One of his flight commanders, Flt Lt Peter Wykeham-Barnes, claimed an SM.79 for his 12th kill that same day. On the 7th Flg Off 'Jas' Storrar of No 73 shot down a CR.42 to score his first victory over Africa. Three days later Flg Off 'Imshi' Mason and Lt Bob Talbot of No 274 were successful over Martuba, the latter becoming an ace.

By the end of January Mason had emerged as the most successful pilot of this first Libyan campaign. Tobruk and Derna had then been captured and No 3 Sqn RAAF had begun re-equipping with Hurricanes. Ominously, however, the first elements of the Luftwaffe had arrived in Libya followed by the advanced elements of Gen Erwin Rommel's *Afrika Korps*.

The Luftwaffe soon began operations, and on 15 February Flg Off John Saunders of No 3 Sqn RAAF shot down a Ju 88 of II./LG 1 to claim the first fighter success against the Luftwaffe in North Africa. Two days later No 3 moved to Tobruk to operate alongside No 73 Sqn, and from there three of them bounced a dozen Ju 87s of II./StG 2 near Mersa Matruh on the 18th. Flg Off John Jackson claimed three destroyed, as did Flt Lt Gordon Steege, who became No 3's second ace, while John Saunders claimed two more. The following day Flt Lt Jock Perrin and Flg Offs Gatward and Boyd encountered the enemy over Agedabia. Perrin dived and shot down Ju 87 Wk-Nr 5455 of II./StG 2, flown by Unteroffizier

The leading ace of the first Libyan campaign was Flg Off 'Imshi' Mason of No 274 Sqn, who added eight aircraft to his score during January 1941. Ever unconventional, he is seen here wearing a very non-regulation goatee beard (*P H Dunn*)

Wt Off Tom Morris of No 274 Sqn sits at readiness in his Hurricane during 1941. He was awarded a DFC on 22 August, having become an ace the previous January (*G R Pitchfork*)

Stuber. Four Bf 110s of 8./ZG 26 then attacked, killing Gatward and hitting Perrin, although he managed to bring down Leutnant Wehmeyer's Bf 110 crash-landing his burning Hurricane. This gallant action earned him an immediate DFC.

There was sporadic action over the next month, particularly around Tobruk, but in late March a German reconnaissance in force resulted in Commonwealth troops beginning a full retreat. No 3 Sqn withdrew too, but on the afternoon of 3 April, as the German advance gathered momentum, its Hurricanes, and four fron No 73, bounced eight Stukas of II./StG 2, and their 7./ZG 26 Bf 110 escorts led by Hauptmann Georg Christl. Flt Lt Alan Rawlinson's section went for the Stukas, while Flt Lt Gordon Steege led Flg Offs Jackson, Saunders and Turnbull against the escort. Peter Turnbull was later credited with four Bf 110s, another went to Gordon Steege, while Rawlinson claimed two Ju 87s – his only victories flying the Hurricane.

The youthful Turnbull was well-regard by his CO, who said that he was 'quick to learn fighter tactics, was quick to the kill, and was able and courageous in leadership'. That was high praise considering the amount of talent then within No 3 Sqn. Two days later, over the Barce Pass, Nos 3 and 73 Sqns gave the hapless Stukas of 4./StG 2 a mauling. Among others, Jock Perrin was credited with three destroyed to become No 3's sole Hurricane-only ace. John Jackson, having shot at several, made his final Hurricane kill. He described the event in his journal;

'I had got on the tail of a fourth and had given it a couple of bursts and silenced its gunner when my guns ceased to fire. So I made a couple of dummy attacks and, much to my delight, he crash-landed in a cultivated wadi.'

There was heavy fighting as the enemy advanced on Tobruk, and when the Germans began their first assault on 11 April Alfred Marshall noted, 'Scramble for dive-bombers. Destroyed one G.50 – crashed on beach west of Tobruk. This enemy aircraft was one of four which attacked me'. As usual, the defenders were outnumbered. On 15 April No 274 Sqn returned to action from Gerawla, but the enemy were soon on the Egyptian border, isolating Tobruk.

The most successful Hurricane pilot of No 3 Sqn RAAF was Flt Lt Jock Perrin, who claimed five of his six victories on the type (*B Cull*)

Hurricane I P3967/OS-B of No 3 Sqn RAAF was flown by Jock Perrin when he brought down three Ju 87s of II./StG 2 on 5 April 1941. Two days earlier fellow ace Flt Lt Gordon Steege was flying this very machine when he shot down a Bf 110 (*Neil Mackenzie*)

These three Free French pilots, attached to No 73 Sqn during the defence of Tobruk, all enjoyed considerable success. They are, from left to right, *Sous Lt* Albert Littolf (seven victories and eight shared), *'Cne* Jean Tulsane (three) and *Sous Lt* James Denis (8.5) (*B Cull*)

The air fighting soon became more hazardous with the appearance of Bf 109s, as Flg Off Dickie Martin of No 73 Sqn quickly discovered. On the 22nd he made his fifth successful claim, an event he described especially for this volume;

'All I can remember of the shooting down of the Hs 126 is that I used all my ammunition on it as it was such a slow and manoeuvrable target. The pilot managed to crashland it successfully and we refrained from shooting up the survivors. The word must have got around, as the next day I was shot down and had to bale out. While I was lying in the sand with a busted shoulder, the Bf 109 pilot who did me made a run over me but held his fire.'

Martin had been flying V7810/TP-W, and was possibly been hit by Oberleutnant Ludwig Franzisket of JG 27. Sqn Ldr Wykeham-Barnes also baled out, although Free French ace *Sous Lt* Albert Littolf claimed his second victory while flying the Hurricane. During May further Hurricane units arrived in Egypt, including No 1 Sqn SAAF from East Africa, and Nos 213 and 229 Sqns from the UK.

SEE-SAW BATTLES

No 1 SAAF was thrown into action in time for Operation *Brevity*, which began on 15 May, but was swiftly stopped by a counter-attack. Both Nos 274 and 1 SAAF Sqns flew extensively, as recounted in the latter's diary for the 16th, 'At approximately 0930, west of El Adem, Lt Talbot shot down a Ju 87. The enemy aircraft was flying at about 200 ft. While still unobserved, Lt Talbot delivered a head-on attack which set the Junkers on fire. The gunner of the enemy aircraft opened up and maintained fire as the aircraft crashed'. Talbot was killed in action soon afterwards.

Meanwhile, No 274 Sqn was hit by Bf 109s and it lost two pilots, including nine-victory ace Flg Off Noel Agazarian. Despite the relative stalemate on the ground, air action continued unabated. No 1 SAAF's diary recounted one victory for rising star Lt A J 'Attie' Botha;

'Lt Botha encountered a Henschel which was flying towards him at 600-700 ft, about 15 miles east of Sidi Rezegh. The enemy aircraft took evasive action in a dive to the deck but after one beam attack by Lt Botha it bunted, crashed and burst into flames.'

By mid-June preparations to relieve Tobruk were complete, and Operation *Battleaxe* began at dawn on the 14th. On its first mission, No 73 Sqn lost three pilots, including Flg Off George Goodman, who was then one of the leading aces in the desert. Patrols were flown throughout the day, during which Capt Ken Driver of No 1 Sqn SAAF (the leading pilot in East Africa) was shot down by I./JG 27's Oberleutnant Franzisket and captured. That evening 20-year-old 'Attie' Botha destroyed two Ju 87s to

**Plt Off John Sowrey of No 213 Sqn
sits in the cockpit of W9349 at
Nicosia in October 1941. He became
an ace the following June during the
heavy desert fighting (*J A Sowrey*)**

become an ace, but he did not have long to enjoy his new status as he was then bounced by Bf 109s and killed.

Among those in action was Flg Off John Sowrey of No 213 Sqn, who recently told the author about his first victory;

'On 15 June I was ordered to patrol the Sollum area and took off with my No 2. We had the sea on our right and were making for Sollum in the haze of the desert air when I saw a pair of Bf 109s below and to our right going in roughly the same direction. I immediately dived to attack. I don't think we were seen as the enemy aircraft took no evasive action. I fired a longish burst into the rear of the two aircraft and pulled away as I was overshooting. I next saw the aircraft explode as it hit the ground and a pall of black smoke went up into the air.'

His victim was probably Feldwebel Schadlisc of 2(H)./14. John Sowrey continued;

'Later that same day, I was again detailed to patrol the Sollum area, where we ran into three or four Bf 109s and the usual melee ensued. I managed to get in some deflection shooting, and felt confident that I had hit one or more of the enemy aircraft, but as the fighting was so confused I couldn't follow the result. However, I recall seeing two aircraft burning on the ground as we left. We had one pilot missing, and I claimed one Bf 109 probable which was later confirmed. My log book says that Plt Off Logan baled out but failed to pull his ripcord.'

Older hands also returned to action, including Flt Lt Vernon Woodward who was attached to No 274 Sqn. He claimed his penultimate victory on the 17th when downed a G.50 of 51° *Stormo* – two more Fiat fighters fell to Sgt Eric Genders. By then heavy tank losses had forced a withdrawal, initially to Capuzzo then Sidi Barrani, before a period of stalemate ensued.

In the air, however, there were often fierce fights, especially over convoys supporting the Tobruk garrison. To increase cover to coastal shipping, the Royal Navy Fighter Squadron (RNFS) was formed, with 16 Hurricanes, from 803 and 806 NASs, while 805 NAS flew Martlets. By August the unit was at Sidi Haneish, and at this same time No 30 Sqn also became operational on Hurricanes at Edku, in the Canal Zone. The latter unit made a big impact when opposing a raid on 7/8 August, bringing down four unidentified aircraft. One fell to Canadian Flt Lt R T P Davidson who, as 'Resta 4', scrambled at 2234 hrs, and later wrote;

'At approximately 2307 I called "Tally Ho!" as a small light was spotted coming towards me, 500 ft below, and about half way down the patrol line. I did a fairly steep turn and positioned behind the enemy aircraft. When about 150 yards away, I fired a fairly long burst directly astern. The aircraft then dropped very rapidly, but flying slow, turned from side to side and I continued to spray the enemy aircraft down to 4000-5000 ft.

Hurricane I Z4244/H was regularly flown by Lt H P Allingham of 806 NAS, which was in turn part of the RNFS. He used it on 21 August when he destroyed a Bf 109, and was again flying it on 1 December when he shot down a Ju 87 and a G.50 (*H P Allingham*)

All-black Hurricane I W9291/M, seen at Edku in August 1941, was used by No 30 Sqn for night defence of the Canal Zone. It was flown by several of the unit's successful pilots, including Flt Lt R T P Davidson, who had an inconclusive night encounter with an enemy aircraft just south of the base on 31 August (*J Hamlin*)

Piraticaly-bearded Flt Lt Bob Davidson became an ace flying with No 30 Sqn in three theatres, namely Greece, North Africa and Ceylon (*D A Macdonald*)

I broke away at this height as AA was opening up at both of us. I then turned sharply and went back on the patrol line'.

His third victim was thought to have been a Ju 88 of 3./LG 1.

The arrival of the improved Bf 109F gave the Luftwaffe a distinct edge, especially in the hands of such skilled pilots as Leutnant Hans-Joachim Marseille. Men like him were a constant threat as the build up to Operation *Crusader* continued. Nine Hurricane fighter squadrons were available when the offensive began on 18 November. Amongst the many new pilot seeing action for the first time was young American volunteer Plt Off Lance Wade of No 33 Sqn. During an attack on El Eng he destroyed two CR.42s, and within a week he had become an ace.

During heavy aerial fighting on the 20th, Sub Lt P N Charlton of the RNFS enjoyed great success near Bir el Gobi when the squadron spotted a dozen escorted Ju 87s from I./StG 2. Flying W9327/M, Charlton went straight for the dive-bombers and shot down three. However, he was then attacked and forced down – by a Tomahawk! Nonetheless, he became the Royal Navy's latest ace, and was later awarded the DFC by the RAF.

Fighting intensified into some of the fiercest clashes of the entire desert war, with the air action of 1 December being typical of the period. Around midday, Nos 1 SAAF and 274 Sqns were escorting a bombing

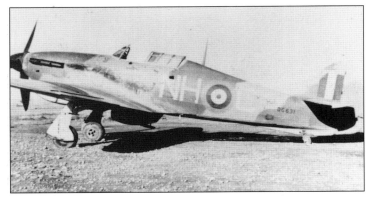

Hurricane IIA DG631/NH-C of No 274 Sqn was flown in combat several times in early February 1942 by Flg Off Wally Conrad, who would eventually score a total of five victories and three shared kills (C H Thomas)

Standing wearing a life jacket is Sgt Hamish Dodds of No 274 Sqn who, with 13 victories and six probables, was the most successful Hurricane pilot in North Africa (author's collection)

raid when they were engaged by Bf 109s and G.50s over El Duda. Four Hurricanes fell, although Plt Off Wally Conrad and Sgt 'Hamish' Dodds each shot down a Bf 109 to claim their first victories. Subsequently downing a further 13 aircraft, Dodds was destined to become the highest-scoring Hurricane pilot of the desert war.

The Hurricanes were constantly in action, and here Maj 'Bennie' Osler, CO of No 1 Sqn SAAF, vividly describes a combat that he was involved in on 7 December;

'I saw a formation of enemy fighters and bombers some 5000 ft below. At this moment I discovered the top cover of Bf 109s positioning themselves to deliver an attack upon our formation. One of these fighters was engaged by myself, and after three short bursts delivered from full beam starboard, three-quarters port astern and line astern slightly low, the C.202, which had already commenced to smoke from the second attack, when subjected to the third simply nosed over into a practically vertical dive earthwards until it impacted and exploded.'

This was Osler's fifth victory. The next day Tobruk was finally relieved. Gradually, the Allies moved toward the Gazala line, but the outbreak of war in the Far East meant many reinforcements being diverted from the desert. A few days later Flg Off O J Hanbury of No 260 Sqn destroyed a Ju 88 near Gazala (his only Hurricane victory), making him an ace.

By mid January the advance was well into Cyrenaica, thus lengthening supply lines. During a convoy patrol on the 17th, Sgt Tom Paxton of No 30 Sqn flew a successful patrol, as he described in his combat report;

'I saw a Ju 88 above and climbed to 10,000 ft. A second enemy aircraft was bombing from 8000 ft, so I immediately chased this machine, keeping in-sun until I got in position for a beam attack. Got an easy burst in form 100 yards and went back into the sun. I waited until the Ju 88 stopped spiral dives, stall turns etc and made a second attack. An explosion occurred in the port mainplane between the engine and the fuselage, and the engine seemed to blow up. It rolled onto its back and fell into ten-tenths cloud below and was confirmed by HMS *Carlisle*.'

Four days later Axis forces began a limited advance, causing the weakened Allied forces to fall back in an effort to try to stabilise the front. On the 24th No 274 Sqn, led by Sqn Ldr Sid Linnard, met Stukas and fighters over Msus. Linnard downed a bomber to score his fifth kill, while Sgt Hamish Dodds also became an ace during the same combat. The mercurial Rommel, however, pushed on towards the Gazala line, the area where many Hurricane squadrons were based. Concentrated ground attacks inflicted significant losses, but poor weather significantly hampered operations well into March.

Hurricane IIB Z5435 of No 274 Sqn as it appeared in the Bir Hacheim area following a force-landing by Sgt Hamish Dodds on 15 May 1942 after being hit by flak during an escort sortie. The machine had been used by fellow ace Flg Off Dudley Honor to bring down a Macchi C.202 on 6 December 1941 (*M R Ford-Jones*)

ALAMEIN BATTLES

The enemy offensive against the Gazala-Bir Hacheim line began on 26 May 1942. It opened a period of heavy fighting which lead eventually to a retreat back to El Alamein. Fighting in the air was intense, especially that in support of the Free French garrison at Bir Hachiem in early June. Among the units involved was No 213 Sqn, as Flg Off John Sowrey recalled to the author;

'We were based at Gazala, and in action practically every day. I see that on 10 June we intercepted 20+ Ju 87s, with a Bf 109 escort. The Hurricane IIC was so inferior to the Bf 109Fs and Gs we were encountering that we evolved what we called a "defensive circle" for self-protection. So here we were going round and round while the Ju 87s were at liberty to bomb our troops. Impetuously, I broke away on my own and attacked the rear of the Ju 87 formation, shooting down a Stuka, and then dived for the deck, and what I thought was home. I was chased by two Bf 109s, crashed in the desert, was strafed on the ground and then, when all was quiet, started walking towards our , which I managed to reach. I was on operations again the next day.'

This eventful sortie resulted in John Sowrey joining the elite band of aces, as did his colleague, Plt Off John Hancock. He also shot down a Stuka, but force-landed and was wounded. The Allies soon began to withdraw from Gazala, with squadrons leapfrogging back to maintain air cover. But Tobruk, so long a symbol of defiance, fell on 21 June. The air

fighting reached a crescendo towards the end of the month as a new line was established at El Alamein.

The Axis assault began on 1 July, and the following day, south-west of Alamein, No 1 Sqn SAAF's Hurricanes fought a pitched battle which was recorded by the unit's Intelligence Officer, Great War pilot 'Pops' Vos;

'At 1840 the order to scramble came and 11 aircraft took off. Fifteen Stukas in three vics of five, with fighter escort, which were peeling off to bomb as the squadron came in from the starboard. Maj "Lemmie" Le Mesurier was the first to draw blood. He delivered a short quarter stern attack. The Stuka blew up completely, and individual attacks were now taking place all over the sky. Capt Peter Metelerkamp, leader of Yellow Section, dived on the tail of a Stuka, firing short bursts. The bomber half rolled and exploded. He got in a burst on another at 50 yards range and this too hit the ground. Peter attacked a third, saw pieces fly off but was then engaged by a Bf 109.'

These were the first of Metelerkamp's five victories. Vos described many actions, and wrote of another colleague;

'Little Harry Gaynor, who had never before fired his guns in anger, was thrilled as they went down on the Stukas. Harry selected his own victim, and was even more thrilled to see it break up into a ball of flame. It was his first victory, and after landing was so overcome that he could scarcely speak.'

Despite the inevitable over-claiming, it was a stunning success for the South Africans, who all paid tribute to Le Mesurier's brilliant leadership.

Heavy fighting continued through July until the enemy was halted and the exhausted armies rested and re-equipped. At the end of August Rommel began his final offensive. He was repulsed at Alam Halfa, although the Bf 109s remained predatory.

On 1 September Marseille, the Luftwaffe's 'Star of Africa', claimed no fewer than 17 fighters shot down. His presence preyed on the minds of many Allied pilots, and the comment of No 213 Sqn's Plt Off Bert Houle's was typical. 'He was an extremely skilled pilot and a deadly shot. It was a helpless feeling to be continually bounced, and to do so little about it'. Within days, however, Rommel's forces began withdrawing

Capt Harry Gaynor of No 1 Sqn SAAF closes up in Hurricane IIC HL627/AX-X over Derna in September 1942 when the squadron was flying from LG 92. He had several successes to his name, and became an ace after the squadron converted to Spitfires (*S A Finney*)

Hurricane IIC BE643/AK-U of No 213 Sqn wears the unit's distinctive 'hornet' roundel. It was flown from Edku on several occasions in April 1942 by Canadian ace Plt Off Bert Houle (*F A W J Wilson via M Lavigne*)

Plt Off Bert Houle of No 213 Sqn is seen here soon after scoring his first victory on the evening of 1 September 1942. He was flying BN231/AK-Y when he shot down a Ju 88 (*A U Houle*)

while the Allies began preparations for their own offensive, which was to prove decisive.

The El Alamein offensive began at 2140 hrs on 23 October, with air operations commencing at dawn the next day. Aircraft were charged with breaking up Axis concentrations, and the action was intense. Late on the 26th, No 213 Sqn headed to intercept a formation of Ju 87s flying low over the coast. Leading one section was Plt Off Bert Houle in HL887/AK-W. He reported;

'For ten minutes nothing showed up. Then a Stuka appeared at 11 o'clock, above. The skyline suddenly seemed to come alive with dots. I closed in on the first one to within 50 yards, stayed slightly below, and gave it both cannon. Large pieces blew off. Then the Stuka belched smoke, turned on its back and went straight down. I veered slightly to starboard where there was another Stuka. I poured cannon fire into it. Its nose dipped slowly and it started to go down in a gentle glide. I followed, giving it an odd burst, until it hit the sea.

'Pulling up behind another, I was able to give it a short squirt, knocking pieces off before it too went over and down. Just over the coast a Stuka put on its navigation lights to show it was friendly. I wasn't, and pulled right in behind it. The outcome was spectacular – high explosive incendiary bullets hit one wing tank and the Stuka became a blazing inferno. I saw the pilot and gunner shrinking to the port side to avoid the heat as it went into a slow right spiral, then hit a spit of land and exploded. I was mesmerised by the suddenness and finality of it all. I attacked another Stuka ahead of me and blew a few pieces off it. I was credited with two destroyed, one probable and two damaged.'

His victims were probably the Ju 87Ds of *Stab* III./StG 3, flown by Hauptmann Kurt Walter, the *Gruppenkommandeur*, and Oberleutnant Karl Lindarfer. Houle, who soon became an ace, received a DFC for this action.

After heavy fighting, the enemy finally cracked and began to withdraw, allowing a general break out on 4 November. Ten days later Nos 213 and 238 Sqns, operating as a makeshift wing, moved to LG 125, behind the enemy's frontline, to harry the retreating Axis forces. The initial strikes came as a complete surprise, and over the next two days the wing took a huge toll of enemy mechanised transport. Increasingly, ground attack became the principle task for the Hurricane units, which continued to support the advance of the Eighth Army through to its final victory in Tunisia. Although obsolete in Europe, the Hurricane had formed the backbone of the Western Desert Air Force for much of the campaign.

OPERATION *TORCH*

Thousands of miles to the west, the Anglo-American landings in Algeria and Morocco, codenamed Operation *Torch,* began on 8 November 1942. Embarked on Royal Navy carriers were the Sea Hurricanes of 802 and 883(HMS *Avenger*), 804 and 891 (HMS *Dasher*) and 800 NASs (HMS *Biter*). 804 NAS's CO was Lt Cdr Jackie Sewell, who had about 13 victories to his credit, while 800 NAS was under the command of the seven-victory ace Lt Cdr Bill Bruen.

The latter unit provided close escort to the first Albacore strike against the French airfields at Oran, *Dasher's* aircraft flying top cover as opposition was expected from the Vichy-French Dewoitine D.520s of GC III/3. In the darkness, 800 NAS located its charges, but the top cover was a shambles as *Dasher's* squadrons were not fully worked up. Over the target fighters were seen, as Sub Lt Mike Crosley recalled;

'There were about ten of them silhouetted against the light sky. Then one or two of the leaders started to fire, so I turned sharp right and saw another yellow looking aircraft on my port quarter above me. By pulling hard on the stick I was able to out turn the chap shooting at me, and after two more complete turns I was beautifully on his tail, closing in on him all the while. After no more than a touch on the button I saw yellow flames coming from his exhausts. Almost immediately I saw the pilot climb out of the cockpit and fall away. The D.520 dived straight in and that was that.

'I took violent evasive action in case any "Froggies" were on my tail. Next I saw a yellow painted job following a Hurricane, and I got him more or less in my sights, closing in under and behind to get a good shot at him before he saw me. He turned too late, and nowhere near steeply enough. I turned well inside him and I couldn't miss. He stupidly reversed his turn during the fight and made it even easier to get on his tail. This one only took another half-second burst, if that. He too disappeared

Suitably bedecked in US markings for the landings in Algeria on 8 November 1942, Sea Hurricane IB JS355 of 800 NAS waits on the deck of HMS *Biter*. It was used by Lt Cdr J M Bruen to shoot down a Dewotine D.520 over La Senia airfield, this kill being his eighth, and final, victory (*J Scutts*)

in a yellow flash of flames as his whole aircraft blew up, 100 yards in front of me. The pilot didn't seem to get out this time and he crashed like the first, just north of the airfield.'

Crosley received a DSC for his actions, becoming an ace over Normandy in 1944. Lt Cdr Bruen also brought down a D.520 for his eighth, and final, kill, as did Sub Lt 'Jock' Ritchie for his fourth victory.

Soon afterwards RAF squadrons began flying in from Gibraltar, including No 43 Sqn, commanded by Sqn Ldr Mickey Rook in HV409/FT-O. He led 'A' Flight down on to Maison Blanche airfield, in Algiers, which was displaying a captured signal. Refuelled, No 43 then mounted a standing patrol for the rest of the day.

The Hurricane units saw only occasional air combat, and only a few pilots increased their scores. One was No 323 Wing leader, Wg Cdr M G F Pedley, who had been the first to land at Maison Blanche. He was leading a patrol at dusk on 12 November, covering paratroopers east of Bougie, when he intercepted a force of bombers and shot down a Ju 88 and an He 111. The latter was his fifth victory, making Pedley the only Hurricane ace of Operation *Torch*.

EAST AFRICA

In East Africa, campaigns to capture Italian colonies in Somaliland and Eritrea and occupied Ethiopia had been launched in late 1940 from the Sudan and Kenya. The SAAF had a sizeable force based in Kenya, including No 3 Sqn at Nairobi and elsewhere with Hurricanes. Supporting the British from the Sudan was No 1 Sqn, based at Azzoza and Port Sudan. It flew Hurricanes and Gladiators, and was commanded by Maj Laurie Wilmot, who later became a wing leader with 4.5 victories.

In mid-January 1941 an offensive began from Kenya into Italian Somaliland, followed by a move into Eritrea from the Sudan. The RAF and SAAF were busy in both areas, No 1 Sqn soon moving to Tessebei, which was the first airfield captured in Eritrea. From there it patrolled the sky over the advancing columns. Italian fighters were often encountered, as on the afternoon of 29 January when Wilmot led an attack on Gura airfield. Future ace Lt Ken Driver described how he shot down an SM.79, which he spotted flying very low near Gura aerodrome;

'I commenced a diving attack and he turned north and then west between the mountains, the whole while keeping very low. On account of his height, it was impossible to carry out any attack other than a stern chase. I fired two bursts into his fuselage and then two more at his starboard engine, which then burst into flames. Two of the crew escaped by parachute before the machine crashed six miles west-northwest of Gura aerodrome.'

On 8 February Driver led an offensive patrol over the capital

No 3 Sqn SAAF Hurricanes were identified by the unit's badge worn on the nose (*A J Thorne*)

Hurricane I 285/V of No 1 Sqn SAAF at Port Sudan had been lent to the unit by No 3 Sqn, whose badge it still wears. The machine was flown by several of No 1's notable pilots, including the CO, Maj Laurie Wilmot, and Lt Ken Driver, who shot down an SM.79 while flying it (*A J Thorne*)

No 1 Sqn SAAF's leading pilots in East Africa pose for an unusual group shot in March 1941. They are, from left to right, Capt Andrew Duncan (5.5 kills, including two on Hurricanes), Capt Ken Driver (ten on Hurricanes), Lt Robin Pare (five, including four on Hurricanes), Maj Laurie Wilmot (4.5, with 2.5 in Hurricanes) and Capt 'Piggy' Boyle (5.5, and 2.5 on Hurricanes) (*C F Shores*)

Asmara, where it was bounced by five CR.42s. In the subsequent dog-fight, he put a good burst into one, which crashed. His fifth victory made him the first Commonwealth ace of the East African campaign. Others soon followed. Early on 13 February Wilmot led a patrol over Asmara, where he again encountered CR.42s. Wilmot fired on one whose engine stopped, then Capt 'Piggy' Boyle set it on fire. The share in this victory represented Boyle's fifth success. He described it in his report;

'I saw above a thin layer of cloud an enemy fighter and a Hurricane attacking one another from ahead. After the attack, the enemy half rolled through the cloud. I dived down and carried out a stern attack. The enemy rolled onto his back and I again fired at him from a very short range. Flames were seen coming from the cockpit and the pilot, who appeared badly injured, managed to jump out after several attempts.'

Wilmot, however, was lost on 23 February. He was attacking Makale airfield when he was bounced by the ace Alberto Veronese in a CR.32. He crash-landed, becoming a PoW, and he remained in captivity until the Italian surrender on 30 June 1941. Capt Andrew Duncan then hit Veronese, who baled out wounded. This was the South African's fourth of his eventual 5.5 victories.

February had seen several unsuccessful attempts to breach the massive natural fortress at Keren. On 15 March another assault began in what proved to be the critical battle of the campaign in Eritrea. The depleted *Regia Aeronautica* fighter units resisted fiercely, and often engaged No 1 Sqn SAAF's Hurricanes. On the 21st, for example, a patrol fought CR.42s over Keren, Ken Driver destroying one and Lt Robin Pare sending

another down in flames, the pilot baling out. Pare was then attacked head-on by a third Fiat, and after a dogfight, it crashed north of Keren.

Three days later, as the battle reached its climax, the 22-year-old Pare brought down two more Fiats to become an ace. Keren fell on the 27th, and on the 31st an early patrol to Asmara spotted three SM.79s bombing the advancing troops. Driver forced one of the Savoias down to score his tenth victory, thus making him the leading Commonwealth fighter pilot in East Africa. Asmara fell the following day, and although there was some more hard fighting, the campaign in the north was effectively over. Within days No 1 Sqn SAAF was moving north to Egypt.

From Kenya, Empire forces struck east into Italian Somaliland on 14 January 1941, with No 3 Sqn's Hurricanes operating over the front in support. On 2 February, for example, they strafed Aligape. The Italians responded, and the following day No 3's Hurricanes scrambled several times. On one of these sorties Capt John Frost spotted three Caproni Ca.133s attacking troops around Dif, but each time he approached he was attacked by the escorting CR.42s. Frost put a long burst into one, which pulled up steeply before falling away to explode in the bush. It was his first victory. Turning into the bombers he attacked one, which crash-landed. The second also fell to his fire, while the third, after two bursts, also crashed. All this had taken place before the cheering troops of the Transvaal Scottish, who captured 11 Italian fliers. Later in the day No 3 Sqn, led by Capt Servaas van Breda Theron, escorted SAAF bombers to Kismayu. Over Gobwen he downed a CR.42 for his first victory.

Towards the end of February the advance gained momentum, and the capital Mogadishu fell on the 25th. No 3 supported a rapid advance north into Ethiopia. During a search for two intruders, on 13 March, Lt Venter ran out of fuel and force-landed. Theron was scrambled when two SM.79s appeared, and after a long chase he shot one down over Dogabur. After refuelling, he took off again to search for Venter. Spotting his aircraft, Theron landed alongside and managed to siphon off some fuel. Upon their return, the pair found their airfield under attack, and each shot down a CR.42 (from 413° *Squadriglia*), as Theron later recalled;

'We were coming along at about 2000 ft when we saw Dudley taking off and Fiats attack him. I gave a signal to Venter and opened my throttle and dived on the Fiat as he machine-gunned the troops and six aircraft parked on the aerodrome. I missed him in the first burst, but as he pulled

Dispersed on a Kenyan airfield in early 1941, Hurricane I 289/A of No 3 Sqn was regularly flown by the leading SAAF ace of the war, Capt John E Frost, who made his first claim while flying it on 29 March when he shot down a CR.42 near Diredawa (*SAAF*)

up I got a long burst in as he came over in a loop. He then did a somersault turn and went straight in from about 1000 ft.'

Two days later John Frost had a similar adventure. Over Diredawa No 3 Sqn downed three fighters, including one each by Theron and Frost. Returning that afternoon, Frost was hit by ground fire and force-landed on a satellite strip. Lt R H Kershaw landed and picked up the ace. Recommended for the VC, Kershaw received the DSO.

The advance into southern Ethiopia led to many SAAF units moving forward to Jigigga, No 3 Sqn reaching it by 24 March. The advance towards Addis Ababa continued, and the capital's airfield was raided on 4 April. The following day the city surrendered, and as mopping-up operations began, the SAAF mounted a heavy raid on Dessie airstrip. Escorting the eight Ju 86s were three Hurricanes, led by Theron, who downed one of the three CR.42s which fell. It was his fifth, and final, claim.

Although air fighting began to reduce in intensity, there were still occasional combats, and John Frost claimed his eighth victory on 30 April when he shot down an SM.79. He later served in the desert, where he rose to become the leading SAAF fighter ace of World War 2.

PERIPHERAL ACTIONS

Hurricane units were also involved in most of the small actions around the periphery of Africa and the Middle East. Early on 8 June 1941, Commonwealth forces, supported by Free French units, invaded Syria to eliminate the potential threat from pro-Axis Vichy French forces. Among the RAF units committed to the operation was No 80 Sqn, based in Palestine, with a detachment in Cyprus. Later joined by the fledgling No 260 Sqn, both units conducted a strafing offensive against Vichy airfields.

No 80 Sqn also saw a good deal of air combat, sometimes with mixed results. One of its early priorities was to provide air cover to the Royal

The only victories gained over Cyprus were by Flg Off George Westlake of No 213 Sqn, who is flying the nearest Hurricane I (Z4223/V) in this formation. He shot down a Ju 88 on 18 July and a Cant Z1007 on 26 August. The leading aircraft is Z4201/Z, which was regularly flown during the autumn by future ace Plt Off Bert Houle. Just behind is W9349/E, named *Spirit of Ceylon*, and regularly flown by another future ace, Plt Off John Sowrey (*M Lavigne*)

Flg Off George Westlake celebrates the destruction of the first enemy aircraft over Cyprus on 18 July 1941. It was also his fifth victory (*J A Sowrey*)

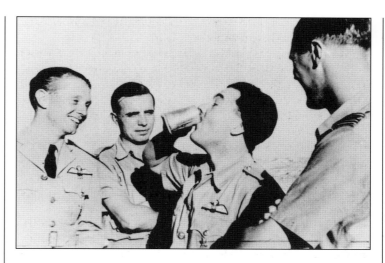

Navy's 15th Cruiser Squadron off the Lebanese coast, which in turn provided gunfire support to advancing troops. These vessels also acted as a magnet to Vichy bombers. That first afternoon Plt Off Roald Dahl attacked a Potez Po 63, which he probably destroyed. A week later he was credited with a Ju 88 destroyed over the force – his fifth claim.

Flg Off Bill Vale was also still flying with the unit at this time, and on 11 June he took off at 0755 hrs on a patrol. He recorded in his log book 'patrol over fleet (one Potez 63)'. The following day he claimed two D.520s, one of which crashed on the coast near Haifa, killing the pilot. He noted '1155: patrol over Fleet (two Dewoitines force landed)'. These were his final victories, and they took his total score to 33 kills, making him one of the most successful, but least known, RAF aces.

An armistice with Vichy authorities in Syria was signed on 12 July, but there was still enemy activity over the eastern Mediterranean. For example, on the 18th No 80 Sqn's detachment in Cyprus was in action when Flg Off George Westlake (detached from No 213 Sqn) intercepted and shot down a Ju 88 off Morphu Bay. His fifth victory attracted great local acclaim, and he repeated the feat the following month by shooting down a Cant Z1007bis. By then the Cyprus unit had been reunited as No 213 Sqn, and Westlake went on to become its most successful pilot of the war.

Further east, there was an Anglo-Russian move against the pro-Axis regime in Iran in August. Operations began on the 25th, with No 261 Sqn's Hurricanes under Sqn Ldr 'Imshi' Mason flying low-level strafing attacks and standing patrols in spite of temperatures reaching 107 degrees. The only air combat of the operation came the next day, and it is described in the squadron record;

'At 8000 ft over Ahwaz the patrol sighted an Audax a thousand below. Sqn Ldr Mason delivered an attack from astern, followed by Sgt Hitchings. No evasive action and the enemy aircraft emitted smoke and went into a glide, landing in a field five miles south east of Ahwaz.'

It was 'Imshi' Mason's 17th, and final, victory. Early on the 28th the fighting ceased.

In West Africa, the British territories of the Gambia and Sierra Leone were surrounded by potentially hostile Vichy French-controlled colonies. Martin 167 bombers from Dakar, in Senegal, were able to reconnoitre the

No 128 Sqn CO Sqn Ldr Billy Drake was victor in one of the few combats fought over West Africa. Here, he admires the nose art on BD897, the aircraft in which he shot down a Vichy French Martin 167 over Sierra Leone on 13 December 1941 (*P H T Green Collection*)

Hurricane IIB BD776/WG-F of No 128 Sqn patrols over the steamy and inhospitable swamps of Sierra Leone. Regularly used by Sgt Arthur Todd, it was also flown in April 1942 by Sqn Ldr John Kilmartin. Its spinner is coloured red, white and blue (*R N Allen*)

anchorage at Freetown, and it was thought that this information was then being passed on to the Germans. Accordingly, in June 1941 the Freetown Defence Flight was organised as part of the resident flying boat unit, No 95 Sqn. One of the original pilots was Battle of Britain ace Flt Lt John Kilmartin. On 22 August Sgt Arthur Todd brought down a Martin near Hastings. The flight duly became No 128 Sqn on 7 October, and a week later its new CO, Sqn Ldr Billy Drake, arrived. He recently told the author that, 'Hastings was a tatty runway from which we took off towards the jungle-covered hills. The unit duties were convoy protection and the defence of Freetown, as well as countering any Vichy reconnaissance aircraft that ventured near.'

Success for the new squadron soon came, and Drake described this rare action in his autobiography;

'They had some Glenn Martin 167F attack bombers at Dakar, which were quite fast and were flown, I understand, by airmen of the French Navy. One of these would occasionally stray into our airspace on a reconnaissance flight. On 13 December 1941 – a Sunday – I had been scrambled on the approach of one such intruder, and was patrolling over the harbour when he appeared. I flew up alongside him and indicated that he should land at our airfield, which he refused to do. This left me with no alternative but to do my stuff and shoot him down – which I did, although I did not like having to do so at all.'

It was his fourth confirmed victory.

There was little further action, and in March 1942 Kilmartin took over, though he too left during the summer. The unit's last action came on 11 October when a Martin 167 was damaged and, following the Vichy surrender in early 1943, No 128 Sqn was disbanded.

JUNGLE FIGHTERS

The Japanese assault in the Far East in early December 1941 caught Allied forces woefully unprepared and poorly equipped. Several Hurricane squadrons were en route overseas at the time of the attack and were hastily diverted. As a result, convoy DM 2, which arrived in Singapore on 13 January 1942, carried 51 crated Hurricanes with 24 pilots from four squadrons – Nos 17, 135, 136 and 232. With No 232's ground party, they became No 232 (Provisional) Sqn under Sqn Ldr L N Landels. The pilots included five future aces and one prime minister-to-be – Plt Off John Gorton RAAF. Unloading and assembling began without delay, and by the 17th 21 Hurricanes were available.

By 20 January No 232 was ready at Seletar. It was just in time, for that same morning came the heaviest Japanese raid on Singapore yet, comprising about 80 bombers, with heavy escort. Amid much optimism, Landels led a dozen Hurricanes to intercept. Sighting the enemy, he dived, but a fighter appeared on his tail and sent him crashing into the sea. He was quickly avenged by his No 2, Sgt Jimmy Parker, who reported later;

'I fell into place about 600 yards behind the pursuing Jap and rapidly overhauled him. He evidently didn't see me and pulled up into a gentle climbing turn as I came into range, still slightly above him. I laid off sufficient deflection, pressed the button and followed the Jap round and up into his turn. I could see my bullets in the air, and was surprised when a myriad of golden flashes appeared sparkling on the nose of the enemy aircraft between the cockpit and the airscrew. The machine turned more sharply to starboard and steeply beneath me and dived away whilst I continued my own swoop into the nearest cloud.'

Lt Yoshio Hatta's Ki-43 'Oscar' of the 64th *Sentai* crashed into the sea close to Landels to become the Hurricane's first Japanese victim. It was also the first of Parker's five confirmed victories. Meanwhile, Flt Lt Edwin Taylor led his section down onto 27 Ki-21s, and they claimed no less than eight destroyed. Taylor himself got two and so did Sgt Sam Hackforth.

During January 1942 Kallang-based No 488 Sqn RNZAF replaced its Brewster Buffalos with Hurricane IIBs. BM899 was amongst the latter aircraft, having been delivered crated as part of convoy DM 2 on the 13th. It was regularly flown by Sqn Ldr J N MacKenzie, who had scored six victories while flying Spitfires in the UK (*RNZAF*)

Others were embroiled with the Ki-43s, and Sgts Henry Nichols and Ron Dovell each shot down one of the Japanese fighters. Two Hurricanes were lost to the highly manoeuvrable 'Oscars', however. That evening Sqn Ldr R E P 'Boy' Brooker DFC, an experienced pilot with four victories, assumed command of the squadron.

The Hurricanes was in action again the following day against Japanese naval aircraft, and although Edwin Taylor downed NAP 1/c Hino's Zero, it was a grim encounter for the unit, which was gaining experience the hard way. On 23 January the 'rookie' No 488 Sqn RNZAF, led by Battle of Britain ace Sqn Ldr John Mackenzie, began swapping its Brewster Buffalos for nine Hurricanes. The change improved morale but the situation remained desperate, with No 232 suffering further losses and a decline in morale among the groundcrews.

On the morning of 26 January a Japanese convoy under heavy escort was spotted approaching Endau, on the east coast of Malaya. All available strike aircraft were ordered to attack, and among the escorts for the first wave were No 232's nine available Hurricanes, led by 'Boy' Brooker. Approaching Endau, the ancient Vildebeeste biplanes began to take losses from flak and Ki-27 'Nate' fighters as the escorts tried to intervene. Brooker downed the nearest for his fifth kill, and Edwin Taylor, Plt Off Jimmy Parker and Sgt Henry Nichols each claimed single 'Nates' as well.

Following his leader down, Sgt Ron Dovell spotted a Ki-27 climbing up. He reported that 'as he was on top of a turn I gave him a short burst. Flames came from the engine and he went down with his engine blazing'. He disengaged and was climbing when he spotted another. 'I must have surprised him, because he made no attempt to get away', he said. 'I gave him a long burst and he went down in an absolutely vertical spin from low altitude. He couldn't have had a hope'. All of No 232's aircraft returned to Singapore, where a second strike was prepared, but it departed ahead of much of the fighter escort.

When it arrived at Endau, Japanese fighters immediately pounced on the force, and although No 232's Hurricanes waded into the enemy, the Vildebeese formation had been destroyed. Sgt Henry Nicholls claimed his second 'Nate', but the day belonged to his friend, Ron Dovell. He chased one Ki-27 at low level and brought it down, before attacking a second with the same result. He had become the first Hurricane ace in the Far East. He received a DFM for his actions, but there was no hiding the fact that it had been a disastrous day for the RAF.

The following day 48 Hurricanes of the original No 232 Sqn, plus No 258, left HMS *Indomitable* for the Dutch East Indies. At Singapore, only 21 of the original aircraft remained available, and with Japanese raids continuing, 12 from No 258 Sqn flew up to Tengah, on the western side of Singapore island. Edwin Taylor became an ace on the 30th, but by then the airfields were barely tenable. At dawn on the 31st the causeway to the mainland was blown up. Later, Flt Lt Denny Sharp led No 258's first scramble against a bomber formation, but over Johore they were engaged by the Ki-43 escort. Two went for Plt Off 'Red' Campbell, a US 'Eagle' volunteer, and he fired on one at close range, as he later excitedly told his fellow American, Plt Off Art Donahue;

'I got a fighter Art. Boy, did we have a party! I saw two fighters coming at me – little chubby fellows with great big radial engines in front and

Hurricane IIB BE163 of No 258 Sqn, which ran into a storm drain at Seletar, seems to illustrate the malaise evident in Singapore in early 1942. It is believed to have been the aircraft regularly flown by one of the volunteer American pilots on the unit, Battle of Britain veteran Flg Off Art Donahue (*A G Donahue*)

Hurricane IIB BE332, seen at Tjililitan, Java, belonged to 'A' Flight of the reconstituted No 605 Sqn. On 25 February 1942 American volunteer Plt Off 'Red' Campbell shot down a Zero with this machine for his fourth victory. Moments later he was himself hit and forced to bale out. Campbell spent the rest of the war as a PoW (*C T R Kelly*)

painted bright green all over. I got well above them and then turned and dived on the nearest one. I got real close before I let him have it. Honest, you never saw anything like it. His machine just seemed to explode with pieces flying off and smoke pouring out. The last I saw of him he was just a ball of fire going down.'

This was the first of Campbell's five claims, four of which were confirmed. But No 258 Sqn lost four of its precious aircraft, and with the airfields now coming under shell fire, it was decided to evacuate most of the remaining fighters to the Dutch East Indies. No 232(P) Sqn and No 488 then left for P1 at Palembang, Sumatra, to counter the increasing Japanese raids. The 'scratch' No 232 Sqn had achieved 38 confirmed victories in 11 days of action.

Coming the other way were some of the 'original' members of No 232 Sqn, led by the experienced Flt Lt 'Ricky' Wright DFM. They were soon in action over the doomed city when they tangled with some Ki-27s on 5 February. Wright was hit and damaged his aircraft landing back at base. Later, Sgt Jimmy King was credited with one of the two G4Ms shot down that day. On the 6th No 232 Sqn lost its CO, and Ricky Wright was promoted to assume command. In more fighting on the 8th Sgt James Sandeman Allen in Z5667/T scored his first victory. He reported, 'I jumped three Army 97s (Ki-21s). The first went into cloud on fire with a dead gunner, while the other two I was able to hit, but I was then forced away by Zeros'. He was soon to become the most successful

Flt Lt Ricky Wright of No 232 Sqn stands in front of BE206/O, which he had force-landed at Kallang on the morning of 5 February 1942. A successful ace, he took command of the squadron, but became a PoW when Java fell (*G Beachamp*)

Cornishman Sgt Henry Nicholls (seated in the front row, centre) achieved six victories over the Japanese while flying with No 232 Sqn. His final two were claimed on 13 February 1942, but he was shot down during the same combat and was evacuated to India, where he later flew Mohawks (*via C H Thomas*)

fighter pilot of the campaign. That night the Japanese crossed from Johore to Singapore, and by dawn some 10,000 men were ashore. On the 10th Kallang was evacuated and the fortress surrendered on the 15th.

— DESTRUCTION IN THE EAST INDIES —

Meanwhile, on 8 February, Palembang was attacked for the third day in succession. Flt Lt Taylor, in BE115, and Sgt Hackforth, in BE219, were the only Hurricane pilots airborne, and in spite of the overwhelming odds they swept into attack. Both were shot down and killed, although Taylor is believed to have accounted for an 'Oscar' and Hackforth got a proba-

ble. Their loss was a severe blow, Taylor having gained six victories and Hackforth four. On Friday 13 February a patrol returned low on fuel to P1 at the same time as a Japanese raid began – the lack of an effective warning system severely hampered the defenders.

Sgt Henry Nicholls gallantly remained to cover his colleagues and was credited with two Ki-43s destroyed. This took his total to six, but he was then forced to bale out and was eventually evacuated to Australia. The next day an invasion fleet appeared and when Japanese paratroops began descending on P1 it was soon overwhelmed. The RAF concentrated at P2, where the Hurricanes flew some effective strafing raids on landing craft moving up the Moesi River. But all serviceable aircraft were soon flown out to Java.

A reorganisation then took place within the Hurricane force, No 232's pilots joining No 242's ground party at Tjililitan, and No 242, under Sqn Ldr Brooker with

No 605 Sqn's fresh ground party, joining Nos 258 and 488 Sqns' pilots to become No 605 under Sqn Ldr Wright. As there were only sufficient aircraft for one squadron, the idea was that they would be flown by each unit in turn. No 242's first action came on the 20th when Flt Lt Ivon Julian destroyed a Ki-27, while No 605 flew its first sorties the next day. With enemy activity over Java increasing, there was further action on the 25th when Sgt 'Sandy' Allen of No 242 Sqn claimed his fifth victory. He reported, 'I was caught by some Zeros. I was claiming damage only to one but Sqn Ldr Wright was in the area and he confirmed the destruction because the 'plane nearly hit him as it went down'.

The Japanese landed in the early hours of 1 March. Allied air forces made strenuous efforts to stop them, but a shortage of aircraft led to No 605's disbandment. From Andir, No 242's patched aircraft continued in action. Jimmy King made his fifth claim on 3 March, and he shot down another two fighters the next day. On the 5th Flt Lt Parker spotted two enemy aircraft near Kalidjati. Later, he reported;

'I had closed to 400 yards, and could see the Japanese insignia. I opened fire and easily followed one round without too much deflection. After a few moments his starboard engine streamed smoke. His nose came up and then he dropped back and dived. I turned away to starboard. When I looked again I saw the parabola of his smoke trail in the sky, and at the end of it, on the ground, a fierce fire where the 'plane was burning.'

Returning to Andir, Parker was attacked by several Zeros but managed to get down safely. The next day Kiwi Sqn Ldr Ivon Julian, now the CO, led a patrol made up of the last six aircraft, his section going to Lembang and Parker taking his to Kalidjati. There, he shot down a bomber for his fifth victory, while Julian too claimed a bomber destroyed over Lembang. This made him the last ace of this ill-fated campaign. After a final reconnaissance on the 8th, the aircraft were destroyed when the Dutch surrendered. Some pilots had remarkable escapes, but most became PoWs, including Jimmy Parker and Ron Dovell, who was later awarded a DFM. In 1946 both Parker and Julian were amongst those to receive the DFC.

With 6.5 victories over Singapore and the East Indies, Sgt Jimmy King was one of the theatre's leading Hurricane aces. He was also fortunate to be one of five fighter pilots to be evacuated on the last aircraft to leave Java for Australia (*via C H Thomas*)

RETREAT FROM BURMA

While elements of some Hurricane squadrons headed for Singapore, three of those en-route to the Middle East were diverted to Burma to form No 267 Wing. Most of the pilots were new, but some were experienced, particularly the squadron COs, Sqn Ldr Bunny Stone (No 17, with three victories and two shared), Sqn Ldr Frank Carey (No 135, with 18 and three shared) and Sqn Ldr Jimmy Elsdon (No 136, with seven victories). The ground crews of Nos 17 and 135 Sqns were ordered to Rangoon to establish servicing facilities, while many of the pilots ferried Hurricanes from the Middle East.

The first four aircraft arrived at Mingaladon, outside Rangoon, on 23 January, and the pilots were immediately ordered to prepare for a strafe on Bangkok because the fixed ferry tanks fitted to their Hurricanes gave them the range to do so. But as they returned from their briefing there was an air raid warning and Elsdon, Stone and two others took off, lugging the fuel tanks with them. Thus encumbered, it was impossible for them to turn with the nimble Ki-27 fighters. Stone's aircraft was badly damaged and he was lucky to escape with his life.

Two Hurricanes of No 135 Sqn are refuelled at Mingaladon in early 1942. On the right is Z5659/WK-C, which was flown by Plt Off Jack Storey in a successful combat over Mingaladon 6 February. He also flew it on the 23rd of that month when he destroyed a 'Nate' for his fourth victory (*W J Storey*)

The next day he and Elsdon scrambled again to encounter half a dozen Ki-21 'Sally' bombers, Stone bringing one down over Rangoon and damaging two more in spite of the fighter escort. Night raids also meant night stand-by duty, which was fatiguing for both pilots and groundcrew. However, on the night of the 27th Stone, in BD921, destroyed another 'Sally', having scrambled with Elsdon. He too had also seen the bombers, and was closing in when Stone's fire appeared over his wing!

No 135 Sqn moved down to Mingaladon on 28 January, and the next day Frank Carey and Plt Off Jack Storey joined in a scramble. Carey shot down his first Japanese aircraft when he destroyed Sgt Maj Nagashima's Ki-27 'Nate'. Storey, the young Australian in his first combat, was soon to make a name for himself. He recalled that first victory;

'I saw three enemy aircraft behind one P-40, which was easily being out-turned. We came down in a steep right-hand spiral at 310 mph this time and selected one enemy aircraft each. I got two steady bursts into mine. Hits were observed and it slipped off into the cloud to the left. Our groundcrews saw an enemy fighter dive out of the cloud and crash near a Blenheim.'

Less than a week later, on 6 February, Storey shot down two 'Nates' in the epic combat illustrated on the cover of this book. At 0900 hrs the following day, a scramble was ordered against an incoming raid on Rangoon. Sgt 'Tex' Barrick, an American volunteer with No 17 Sqn flying BE171/YB-B, downed two Ki-27s, while 'Bojo' Brown of No 136 also claimed his first victory. But with the Japanese crossing the Sittang and Salween rivers in force, it was becoming increasingly evident that Rangoon could not be held. Plans for an evacuation north were laid in the face of increased enemy air activity.

A few days later Frank Carey was promoted to wing commander to lead No 267 Wing. He was replaced as No 135's CO by Sqn Ldr Barry Sutton from No 136, who in turn selected Jack Storey as a flight commander. The reason, Sutton said, was that Storey was 'a pilot of exceptional ability, one of the best leaders of a formation I have ever seen'.

Storey's first victim was this Nakajima Ki-27 of the 77th *Sentai*, which dived into the ground near a parked Blenheim at Mingaladon (*C A C Stone*)

Little was seen of the enemy for the next ten days, giving the defenders a welcome respite until a new offensive began on 21 February. Two days later Carey led a scramble at 0930 hrs, and made his first claim as wing leader when he shot down a 70th Chutai Ki-51 reconnaissance aircraft in flames. One of his protégés, Jack Storey, downed his fourth Ki-27 in the same encounter. Carey also initiated attacks on the enemy airfield at Moulmein, but his squadrons' main task remained the defence of Rangoon. There was a big raid on the 25th, and at noon the first fighter sweep approached. Among those airborne was Tex Barrick in 'YB-O', who had a lucky escape;

'I attacked and shot down one Army 97 and was then jumped from above by a Zero. I went into a tight turn, which caused one of the gun panels to fly open. This made the aircraft flick, and probably saved my life!'

Barry Sutton of No 135 Sqn was delayed due to a starter problem. Once in the air, he was unable to locate the fight and flew over the Gulf of Martuban. He encountered the returning raid over Moulmein and attacked a bomber, which was listed as a probable. He then headed over the Gulf again and encountered a Japanese fighter head-on. 'Never have I had a head-on burst at a fighter' he said later.

'He too is just above the wave tops. We flash past each other much less than a cricket pitch away. He zooms up and behind, now standing on one wing, spread-eagled against the skyline. One minute he is there, the next he is not. He has crashed either because he spun off in a very tight turn or because I had hit him. The latter is the more likely reason, I think.'

Sutton was credited with destroying the fighter, possibly the Ki-27 flown by Lt Mihara of the 50th *Sentai*. It was his fifth, and final, kill.

The following day Frank Carey led another attack on Moulmein, during which he brought down three more 'Nates'. 'They were well committed to their final approach, and I dived down with Underwood and picked off the rearmost of the two', he said later of his first success. 'He fell in a bit of a heap on the end of the runway, which was only to be expected'. These two successes took

Hurricane IIB BE171/YB-B of No 17 Sqn was one of the few desert-camouflaged aircraft to reach Burma, where it is seen at Mingaladon in late January. It was regularly flown by the CO, although he made no claims in it. Sgt 'Tex' Barrick did, however, bringing down two Ki-27s over Rangoon on 7 February – the first of his five victories (*C A C Stone*)

One of the most successful pilots of the Burma campaign was Plt Off Jack Storey, who claimed his first victory on his first operational sortie (*W J Storey*)

his tally to 28 destroyed. Plt Off Guy Underwood baled out and was captured after he had shot a fighter off Carey's tail. Also successful was Flt Lt 'Bush' Cotton of No 17 Sqn, who claimed one of the enemy fighters. During a later scramble after claiming a bomber shot down, he was hit and wounded by one of the escorts. He received an immediate DFC for his courage, while Wg Cdr Carey was soon to receive a second bar to his DFC for his efforts over southern Burma. However, the end was not far off as most RAF units withdrew north to Magwe.

Two wings were established, one at Magwe with Nos 17 and 135 Sqns, and the other at Akyab, comprising No 136 Sqn, supported by elements of No 135. For the former wing, covering the army's withdrawal northward, strafing was the order of the day, but the fall of Rangoon on 8 March transformed the situation in Burma. Offensive sorties continued from Magwe until a massive retaliatory raid on the afternoon of 21 March virtually destroyed what was left of the RAF at Magwe. Even so, Plt Off Hedley Everard downed a 64th *Sentai* Ki-43 for the first of his 5.5 kills.

The following morning the Japanese returned in strength to finish the job. The airfield was evacuated, with most aircraft going to Akyab on the coast. Others, including Tex Barrick, continued to move north until they ended up at Loiwing, in China, in early April. From Akyab many personnel were then moved on to Chittagong, leaving No 136 as the only fighter unit in Burma. The Japanese then turned on Akyab, and the first raid came on the 23rd. Sqn Ldr Elsdon led the scramble but Ki-43s were quickly on them, and Plt Off Brown was forced to bale out with severe burns. The survivors were ordered to withdraw and Akyab was abandoned on the 28th.

The RAF remnants at Loiwing saw some further action, and during the afternoon of 10 April Sgt Barrick shot down a Ki-43 to score his fifth victory. He was, however, attacked by three more and injured in the

The leading pilot of the first Burma campaign, and one of the RAF's most influential fighter leaders of the war, was Wg Cdr Frank Carey. In February 1942 he became OC No 267 Wing (*N L R Franks*)

Flt Lt 'Bush' Cotton leans against his No 17 Sqn Hurricane at Mingaladon on 26 February 1942. This photograph was taken before he had shot down a 'Nate' over Moulmein, and was subsequently badly wounded later that same day. Second from the left is Sgt 'Tex' Barrick, who downed five Japanese fighters during the retreat (*M C C Cotton*)

subsequent forced landing – RAF fighter operations over Burma effectively ended soon afterwards. No 17 Sqn's latest ace rejoined the unit in India, receiving a well-earned DFM and later a commission. He and Carey were the only Hurricane pilots to claim five or more victories during this first Burma campaign, which ended when the last troops reached Imphal in mid May. It had been a long and bitter retreat.

STRIKE ON CEYLON

Following their series of stunning successes throughout the Pacific and South East Asia, the Japanese turned their attention to the Indian Ocean, using their potent carrier striking force. The island of Ceylon was a strategic target thanks to its two superb natural harbours and strategic location lying across the main shipping routes to and from Africa and Australasia. The island's fighter defences were meagre, although there were plans to rectify this. On 1 March 1942 the 'new' Hurricane unit assembled at the Racecourse, Colombo, and was initially named 'K' Sqn, but as former members of No 258 arrived from the East Indies, that designation was used from 30 March. The experienced pilots who joined the squadron included Flt Lt Teddy Peacock-Edwards, who had seen action over the UK and Malta.

Further aircraft arrived on 6 March when No 30 Sqn's Hurricanes flew off HMS *Indomitable* to Ratmalana. The following day No 261 followed suit to China Bay. No 30 was an experienced night flying unit from the desert, and among its successful pilots were Flt Lt Bob Davidson, Plt Off Jimmy Whalen and Flt Sgt Tom Paxton. Each already had three kills. No 261, led by 18-victory ace Sqn Ldr Arthur Lewis, also comprised several experienced pilots including Flt Lt David Fulford with four victories.

Soon after dawn on Easter Sunday the enemy carrier-borne strike on Colombo began. Although expected, there was no immediate early warning, and the attack came as a surprise. Sqn Ldr R J Walker, later No 258 Sqn's CO, recalled to the author the events at the Racecourse that day;

'At the time of the Easter raid on Colombo I was told that the Japs put a standing patrol over Ratmalana to the south, but knew nothing of the Racecourse. The ops room called up dispersal and said, "can you see any aircraft about?" When an affirmative reply was received, they shouted "Well scramble – they're Japs!"'

The Hurricanes clawed for height after the dive-bombers but were attacked by the Zero escort and nine went down, with five pilots killed. Four dive-bombers were claimed, one by Teddy Peacock-Edwards in Z5461/ZT-B. He recalled his final victory;

A stalwart of No 136 Sqn until his death in action in February 1944, Flt Lt Eric 'Bojo' Brown climbs into his Hurricane IIC at Chittagong around May 1943. His final total was four destroyed and one probable (*V K Jacobs*)

The aircraft carrier HMS *Indomitable* played a key role in reinforcing the Far East by bringing RAF Hurricanes to Sumatra and Ceylon as deck cargo in the early months of 1942 (*author's collection*)

No 258 Sqn was reconstituted in Ceylon in March 1942 and saw action during the Japanese strike on Colombo at Easter. Here, one of its Hurricane IIBs (BN125/ZT-R) has suffered a minor accident at Colombo whilst being flown by Plt Off Jock McCulloch. He had escaped after a torrid time in Sumatra and Java. where he had damaged one Ki-43 (*D B F Nichols*)

'We scrambled furiously and I climbed right up after them, catching them up over the sea just as they were turning back towards the harbour. I went down after them and got one from behind in the middle of the dive. Then their fighters came tearing down, and tracer began to fly uncomfortably close round my cockpit.'

Another D3A 'Val' fell to the CO, who was himself hit by a Zero and had to bale out. Both Peacock-Edwards and Walker received the DFC for their actions on this day.

At Ratmalana, No 30 Sqn was being turned around when the enemy formations were spotted. The 21 Hurricanes that were scrambled never had the opportunity to form up, and their resulting attacks were uncoordinated. Flt Lt Bob Davidson found himself in low cloud, but shot down a D3A 'Val' and an escorting Zero to make him an ace. Another of No 30's pilots with several claims from the desert war to his credit was Flt Sgt Tom Paxton. He engaged the enemy attack, shooting down a Zero (probably that of NAP 1/c Higashi from the *Soryu*), before turning into another which he also shot down to take his total to 5.5. But Paxton was hit and forced to bale out of his blazing aircraft, and although he received treatment for burns, he died from shock two days later.

Another successful pilot was Flg Off Alan Wagner, who claimed two 'Vals' – he later became an ace in 1944 flying Mosquito intruders. The most successful, though, was 22-year-old Canadian Flg Off Jimmy Whalen, who shot down three 'Vals' to hoist his total to six. The enemy attack ended soon after 0900 hrs, and although the defenders had suffered heavy losses, they had succeeded in breaking up the cohesion of the raid. Against the loss of eight aircraft, No 30 Sqn claimed 14 destroyed.

The expected further strikes did not materialise until the 9th. This time Trincomalee, on the other side of the island, was the target. Over 100 aircraft were detected at 0700 hrs while a patrol from No 261 Sqn, led by Flt Lt David Fulford, was near the harbour. The Hurricanes engaged the leading Japanese formation as it approached, Fulford closing on a Zero from astern and giving it a five-second burst from very close range. The fighter began to break up and spin, and at a height of 12,000 ft, the starboard wing came away, taking formation leader Lt Masatoshi Makino

Teddy Peacock-Edwards demonstrates how he destroyed a 'Val' dive-bomber over Colombo to gain his final victory (*via J Hamlin*)

Although the defending fighters suffered heavy losses in the raid on Colombo on 5 April 1942, some pilots were successful, including Plt Off Jimmy Whalen of No 30 Sqn. Flying this Hurricane IIB BG827/RS-W, he was credited with destroying three D3A 'Val' dive-bombers, thus elevating him to ace status (*Public Archives of Canada*)

Having made his initial claims at night over England, Plt Off Alan Wagner moved to Ceylon with No 30 Sqn, where he shot down two 'Val' dive-bombers over Colombo on 4 April 1942. He became an ace the following year (*D B F Nichols*)

from the *Zuikaku* to his death. Evading six more Zeros, Fulford spotted a formation leaving the harbour. He dived on the rearmost fighter, firing the rest of his ammunition at it and causing the A6M to turn on to its back and crash into the sea. These were his final claims, and they made him an ace. Others from his section also made claims before they succumbed to the Japanese attack. More Hurricanes scrambled from the airfield, but many fell to the Japanese fighter escorts. One who claimed was Flg Off C F Counter in BE241. He pulled behind an A6M which he hit, causing it to roll and crash into the lagoon. It was one of four victories he would eventually score, but he was then attacked and force-landed under fire at a devastated China Bay.

The CO, Sqn Ldr Arthur Lewis, took off late and had a torrid time. 'I had barely got my undercart up', he said later, 'when a hail of bullets struck the armour plate at my back and the throttle lever was no longer there. Two 'planes with blood red roundels slid by in close formation'. He baled out injured and was repatriated to England soon afterwards. His had been one of eight Hurricanes lost, but No 261 Sqn claimed four bombers and four fighters destroyed. Fortunately for the defenders, the Japanese withdrew, No 261 having been reduced to just six serviceable Hurricanes. The fighter force was, however, soon rebuilt against a possible repeat attack on this vital base. Hurricane fighter squadrons remained on Ceylon for several years, but the Japanese did not return.

THE ARAKAN

The arrival of the monsoon in eastern India in mid 1942 greatly restricted flying operations by the combatants. At airfields around Calcutta, battered units recuperated and were reinforced by the arrival of Nos 79, 607 and 615 Sqns with Hurricanes from the UK. Existing units like Nos 67 and 146 also swapped their Mohawk IVs and Buffalos for Hurricanes.

To increase the visibility of the RAF's presence to the population of Calcutta, No 136 Sqn moved in late June to an improvised strip on the Red Road right in the centre of the city. In fact the road was just wider than the Hurricane's wingspan. Here it remained until August when, after a detachment was sent down the coast, it returned to Dum Dum, Calcutta, to operate alongside No 135 Sqn. As the monsoon ended, the Arakan peninsula – a rugged jungle-covered area running south from the Indian border to the port of Akyab – became the focus of operations for the immediate future. To participate, the Hurricane units would be moved forward to strips around Cox's Bazaar and Chittagong, in East Bengal, from where they could also cover the overland approach of any raids on Calcutta.

The first Japanese air raid after the monsoon came on 22 October 1942 when 30 fighters attacked Chittagong. Complete surprise was achieved, and the attacks were repeated regularly. In return, on the 27th, No 615 Sqn flew its first sweep down the Naf Peninsula, but the Japanese usually husbanded their resources, only moving forward to mount their own operations. However, in December operations intensified, and Chittagong was attacked again on the 10th. The raid was intercepted by Nos 135 and 136 Sqns, which were roughly handled by the escorting 'Oscars'.

On the 14th No 79 relieved No 136 at Chittagong, and the next day the airfield was attacked. Three Ki-48s and two 'Oscars' fell, one of the bombers being shot down south of Chittagong by Flg Off Russ Bowes – as the first of his 5.5 victories over Burma. The raid was the opening attack in a concentrated series of mission flown over the next few days which resulted in some savage dogfights. On the ground, the enemy advanced up the Arakan as far as Maungdaw.

Among the new units formed in India was No 146 Sqn, to which Hurricane IIB BG685/NA-N belonged when pictured here at Dum Dum in July 1942. The squadron was commanded by Battle of Britain ace Sqn Ldr Count Manfred Czernin, who occasionally flew this aircraft (*S Walker*)

The mangled remains of No 17 Sqn Hurricane IIC BN781 after its engine had cut at Alipore on 20 October 1942 while being flown by future ace Plt Off 'Snooks' Everard. The five Japanese victory flags show it to have been the regular aircraft of American ace Wt Off 'Tex' Barrick (*via B Cull*)

On the 20th the RAF hit Magwe airfield, the escort comprising a dozen Hurricanes from No 607 and 615 Sqns. They engaged some 50th *Sentai* 'Oscars', allowing future ace Sgt Wilf Goold to claim his first (and only) Hurricane victory. Of greater significance that night was the first of a series of small-scale night bombing raids on Calcutta, which caused mass panic among the teeming population. Attacks on enemy airfields continued in preparation for a British offensive towards Maungaw and possibly Akyab. There were five Hurricane squadrons available, and over Magwe on Christmas Eve No 607 Sqn's Flt Sgt 'Banger' Yates, in his first action, downed an 'Oscar' and shared in the destruction of a second. Two Hurricanes were lost. Yates later took his score to 4.5 while flying Spitfires.

In early 1943 No 224 Group's squadrons, which were increasingly flying the cannon-armed Hurricane Mk IIC, conducted many attacks over the Mayu against all types of transport, both road and river. There were many losses, however. 'Bojo' Brown of No 136 Sqn led one such attack on 22 January which was briefed by SASO No 224 Group, Gp Capt 'Hank' More, a six-victory ace from the Battle of France. He was shot down over the target to become a PoW, and was later lost at sea while being shipped to Japan. These sorties prompted an increase in Japanese air activity, with attacks flown against airfields and forward positions resulting in several combats. One came on the 23rd when Flt Sgt Bob Cross of No 136 Sqn encountered Ki-43s near Chittagong. He later wrote in his combat report;

'We made a turn to starboard in order to intercept the bombers and were jumped by two Japanese fighters almost immediately. At the moment of attack I was weaving behind Plt Off Adamson. In making an attack on him, one of the

Pilots of No 79 Sqn pose with a visiting dignitary in Calcutta. Third from the right is the squadron's most successful Arakan pilot, Australian Flg Off Russ Bowes, who had claimed 5.5 victories prior to his death in action on 21 May 1943 (*G J C Hogan*)

Hurricane IIN BM913/N, which carries No 136 Sqn's distinctive woodpecker badge, belonged to Flt Lt Eric 'Bojo' Brown. Seen at Chittagong in May 1943, he was flying it on the 22nd when he destroyed a Ki-48 'Lily' (*F W Davis*)

The leading Commonwealth pilot over Burma and South East Asia was Flt Sgt Bob Cross of No 136 Sqn, who scored the first three of his nine victories flying the Hurricane (*V K Jacobs*)

Wearing a mixture of interim markings in mid 1943 is Hurricane IIB AP894/C of No 135 Sqn. Flt Lt Jack Storey shot down four Ki-43 'Oscars' while flying this aircraft between March and May. It was struck off charge on 7 July 1943 (*W J Storey*)

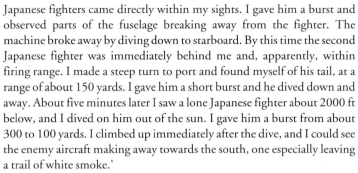

Japanese fighters came directly within my sights. I gave him a burst and observed parts of the fuselage breaking away from the fighter. The machine broke away by diving down to starboard. By this time the second Japanese fighter was immediately behind me and, apparently, within firing range. I made a steep turn to port and found myself of his tail, at a range of about 150 yards. I gave him a short burst and he dived down and away. About five minutes later I saw a lone Japanese fighter about 2000 ft below, and I dived on him out of the sun. I gave him a burst from about 300 to 100 yards. I climbed up immediately after the dive, and I could see the enemy aircraft making away towards the south, one especially leaving a trail of white smoke.'

The RAF's top scorer in Burma had scored his initial victories. Cross's first victim was thought to have been a significant scalp indeed – Maj Shigeru Nakazaki, a nine-victory ace with the 50th *Sentai*. Cross was later credited with the second 'Oscar' that he claimed.

As the enemy was reinforced, the British offensive slowly ground to a halt, and the hope of achieving any of the limited objectives evaporated. The enemy continued to appear in strength, and a patrol from No 136 Sqn was severely handled on 3 February. Other units were also moved forward, including Nos 67 and 261 Sqns, and all continued to see sporadic action. No 135 Sqn had its most successful day on 5 March when 'B' Flight was held readiness at 'George' strip, while 'A' Flight, led by Flt Lt Storey in AP894/C, flew a patrol over Akyab from 'Ritz'. At 21,000 ft they ran into a gaggle of Ki-43 'Oscars', as Jack Storey recalled;

'The Japs split up, and during the dogfight which soon took us down to 12,000 ft, more appeared and joined in. After much tail chasing I finally got an opening and carried out a downward quarter attack on a straggler and got in a beautiful deflection shot – saw de Wilde strikes on the port mainplane, engine, cockpit and tailplane. It rolled over and went straight down through clouds, streaming petrol vapour from the port wing tank. "Hawk" (Flt Lt Lee Hawkins – author) went down immediately afterwards with three Japs on his tail, and said he saw the tail unit of my "Oscar" sticking up out of the water with black smoke coming up from around it.'

Storey led his men back to 'Ritz' to refuel, landing at 1045 hrs when his fifth victory was confirmed. After refuelling, 'A' Flight then escorted a VIP aircraft to India, after which they returned over Akyab at 25,000 ft to seek out the Japanese standing patrol. Storey found that they were well

positioned to jump a vic of 'Oscars' which they had spotted. 'I chose the No 3 and sent him down with quite a short burst from dead astern', he reported. 'He plummeted down, exploding on impact on the north tip of Baronga Island'. His No 2 claimed a second, and as more 'Oscars' arrived, a big fight ensued. Jack Storey again;

'I singled out one lone fighter which seemed to be looking for trouble at 2000 ft below everything.

After taking a good look to ensure no trap existed, I went down after him and got in a good burst which caused pieces to fly off the aircraft. After pulling steeply upwards, I rolled over and was astonished to see the pilot bale out, as this was the first occasion I had actually seen a Jap do this.'

Storey was awarded a well-deserved DFC a month later.

Meanwhile, Nos 79 and 607 Sqns were escorting Blenheims of No 11 Sqn in a raid on Aungdaing, during which they became embroiled with 'Oscars'. No 79 lost one aircraft, but Flg Off Russ Bowes managed to down one in flames as it flew across his nose. It was his second victory.

Sporadic air action continued until the middle of March, when the Japanese Army Air Force withdrew south to prepare for a major air offensive. The RAF also continued to attack Japanese-held airfields, and No 11's Blenhiems were badly mauled over Magwe on the 14th. The following day, Nos 136 and 607 Sqns escorted more bombers, but encountered an in-bound enemy raid. In the subsequent fight four Hurricanes were lost, although Sqn Ldr Alfie Bayne of No 136 scored his 11th victory. It was one of four RAF claims made that day. Bayne was described by one of his pilots as 'a very forthright chap. He wasn't easy to live with, but he was a very good operational leader'. No 79 was scrambled too, and Russ Bowes was able to claim one kill, although his aircraft was damaged.

The heavy ground fighting around Donbaik meant sustained action, and on 27 March 25 Ki-48 'Lilys' attacked Cox's Bazaar, incredibly without escort. Among those scrambled were two sections of No 79 Sqn, led by Bowes, and seven aircraft from No 135 Sqn. In the subsequent fight, most pilots claimed, and Bowes destroyed one 'Lily' and shared in another to become an ace. But the day belonged to Plt Off 'Happy' Armstrong of No 135 Sqn, who was credited with one 'Lily' destroyed and three others shared. The continued bitter air fighting led to significant RAF losses, and on the 31st No 135 suffered three shot down, with others damaged. Armstrong downed a 64th *Sentai* 'Oscar'. He reported;

'I made a starboard quarter attack on an enemy aircraft that was turning slightly to starboard, firing about a four-seconds burst, closing in to about 50 yards. White smoke started coming from the enemy aircraft and I pulled into a steep climbing turn to starboard. The enemy aircraft followed me up, but was left behind. It levelled off and stall-turned, giving me a two- or three-second burst from astern and above. White and black smoke poured out of him and he went down in a very slow flat spin'. The Ki-43 was Armstrong's fifth success in as a many days. It took him rapidly to ace status, but he made no further claims.

The action continued into May 1943, with Flt Sgt Bob Cross again being successful on the 2nd when six from No 136 Sqn scrambled from 'Reindeer' to be joined by four more from Chittagong. In a running fight, Cross brought down a 'Sally', as witnessed by a colleague. 'I saw Bob Cross go down amongst them – he was an amazing fellow', he said. 'When we got back I asked

One of No 136 Sqn's most successful COs was Sqn Ldr Alf Bayne, who claimed his 11th, and last, victory on 15 March 1943 when he shot down a Ki-43 'Oscar' (*D A MacDonald*)

No 79 Sqn's Hurricane IICs were very active during the heavy Arakan fighting of 1942-43. This one, seen parked at Chittagong, retains full UK-style markings (*author's collection*)

Hurricane IIC HW620/HM-E of No 136 Sqn is prepared for a mission at Chittagong in early 1943. Assigned to Flg Off Viv Jacobs, this aircraft was also flown regularly by Flt Sgt Bob Cross, who used it during the incredible combat of 5 April 1943 when he probably destroyed an 'Oscar' and damaged five more. He was also flying this aircraft when he shot down a Ki-21 'Sally' on 2 May (*V K Jacobs*)

With seven enemy aircraft destroyed, including three on Hurricanes over the Arakan in 1943, Plt Off Gordon Conway of No 136 Sqn was one of the leading RAF pilots of the Burma campaign (*A G Conway*)

The Red Road airstrip in the centre of Calcutta was very narrow, and when, on 10 July 1942, Plt Off Conway's aircraft suffered a tyre burst, it collided with an adjacent balustrade (*V K Jacobs*)

how he'd got on, and he replied, "Oh, I blew the wing off a bomber and hit one of the fighters." He was very cool'. Other units suffered, however, with No 146 Sqn being particularly badly hit. Three days later Jack Storey claimed his eighth, and final, victory to make him the most successful Hurricane pilot in the Far East. Losses continued, though. Malta ace Sqn Ldr 'Dimsie' Stones, now with No 67 Sqn, was wounded on the 15th and Flt Lt Bowes of No 79 Sqn was killed on 21 May.

Both Nos 67 and 136 Sqns had some successes the next day, and a week later the latter unit was lucky to intercept another raid on Chittagong. Flg Off Jim Gillies scrambled and shot down a Ki-21 'Sally' and a Ki-43 'Oscar'. They were his only victories against the Japanese, but they made him an ace. Later, he flew on ground attack missions and was awarded a Military Cross for his work with the Army, an unusual decoration for an RAF pilot. Also airborne was Plt Off Gordon Conway, who had cause to remember his final Hurricane victory. 'A Jap turned onto our leader's tail in front of my section', he said. 'I gave this "Oscar" a long burst of cannon and he literally fell apart. He seemed to stop in mid-air. His port wheel came down, as did his flaps, and with pieces flying off all round, he flicked and spun vertically into the sea just by the airfield'. His victim was probably the six-victory ace Sgt Miyoshi Wanatabe.

The coming monsoon, combined with the recent heavy fighting, left both sides exhausted. It also ended the initial Arakan campaign. By the next round, Spitfires would shoulder much of the air combat burden. Although they saw some fighting later in the year, the Hurricane squadrons mainly concentrated on fighter-bomber work for the remainder of the war in Burma. Their pilots had flown with great distinction, often against heavy odds and in the most difficult operating conditions.

EPILOGUE

The battles over the Arakan during 1943 had represented the last large-scale use of the Hurricane as a pure day fighter. But Hurricane squadrons continued to give sterling service in the fighter-bomber role in Burma to the end of the war. And they were occasionally caught up in air combats as well. For example, No 134 Sqn, led by Sqn Ldr Stratton, engaged 'Oscars' over the 'Admin Box' on 8 February 1944, as did No 261 Sqn the day after. More significantly, on the 15th Flg Off Jagdish Chandra Verma of No 6 Sqn Indian Air Force shot down an 'Oscar' to claim the only IAF victory of the war.

The Hurricane remained in service as a fighter-bomber over the Balkans and continued to serve at home as well. In the UK, it was used mainly for second-line tasks, yet it was still occasionally flown by ace pilots. Battle of Britain and North Africa Hurricane ace Sqn Ldr 'Jas' Storrar, for example, flew with No 1687 Flt in mid-1944, delivering high priority mail to the Allied armies in France in the wake of the Normandy invasion, while in September Battle of Britain Spitfire ace Flt Lt J K Norwell became a flight commander with No 527 Sqn, a calibration unit which had several Hurricanes on its strength.

The Sea Hurricane remained operational with the Royal Navy well into 1944, and it would appear that these were the last Hurricanes to score aerial victories. Soon after dawn on 26 May in the Bay of Biscay, Sub Lt Al Burgham of 835 NAS, aboard HMS *Nairana*, used NF672/7K to shoot down Ju 290 '9K+FK' of 2./FAG 5, although his wingman was lost. He recalled the end of the four-engine aircraft;

Radar calibration was the task of No 527 Sqn at Digby, to which Hurricane XII JS290/WN-P belonged when pictured here in 1945. The flight commander was Battle of Britain ace Flt Lt 'Jock' Norwell, who had previously flown Hurricanes over Malta (*RAF Digby*)

Sea Hurricane IIC NF672/7K of 835 NAS suffered this minor accident on HMS *Nairana* on 25 June 1944. The previous month, on 26 May, Sub Lt Burgham was flying this very machine when he shot down a Ju 290 over the Bay of Biscay. That same afternoon its regular pilot, Sub Lt Mearns, shot down a second Ju 290 in another aircraft – the latter is thought to have been the Hurricane's final aerial victim of World War 2 (*via R L Ward*)

'I pressed home my own attack, hitting the Junkers repeatedly at close range. It crashed into the sea and exploded. All that remained of the Junkers was an oil slick and a few floating pieces of debris. It all happened unbelievably quickly.'

Later that afternoon Sub Lts Sam Mearns, at the controls of NF698/7D, and Frank Wallis attacked two more Ju 290s, bringing down '9V+GK' (Wk-Nr 164) of 1./FAG 5 flown by Leutnant Kurt Nonneberg. The huge aircraft broke up on impact, although four of his crew were picked up. It is perhaps appropriate to give the last word to a survivor of the final Hurricane victory. He said;

'We left Mont de Marsan at 1100 hrs, led by Hauptmann Pavletke. Both aircraft were fitted with *Hohentweil* radar, and flew close for mutual protection at about 1000 ft to continue the convoy surveillance. However, after about six-and-a-half hours we were unexpectedly attacked by Hurricanes before we sighted the convoy.

'The tail gunner and rear dorsal gunner opened fire but the latter's gun jammed. In an attack from fine astern, the port inner engine was set on fire and the port wing damaged. The second pilot, who was at the controls, was seriously wounded, whereupon the first pilot took over and ditched the aircraft, in the course of which manoeuvre the tail and port wing struck the water and broke off.'

APPENDICES

Hurricane Aces 1941-45

Name	Service/ Nationality	Kills 1941-45	Total Kills	Sqn/s	Theatre/s
M T StJ Pattle	RAF	35.5/4/1	50+2sh/7.5/4+2sh	80 & 33	Greece
W Vale	RAF	20/1/5	30+3/-/6.5	80	Greece/Syria
K M Kuttelwascher	Czech	18/-/5	18/2/5	1	UK
V C Woodward	RAF	14+3sh/3/11	18+4sh/3/11	33 & 213	ME/Greece
R P Stevens	RAF	14.5/2/1	14.5/2/1	151 & 253	UK
J Dodds	RAF	13/6/8	13/6/8	274	ME
E W F Hewett	RAF	13/2/-	16/2/-	80	Greece
J A F Maclachlan	RAF	13/-/3	16.5/-/3	261 & 1	Malta/UK
L C Wade	RAF	12+2sh/-/4	22+2sh/1/13	33	ME
F N Robertson	RAF	10/3/7	11.5/3/7	261	Malta
E M Mason	RAF	10/-/1	15+2sh/-/3+2sh	274 & 261	ME/Malta/Iran/ME
A C Rabagliati	RAF	9.5/2/3	16.5/4/7	46/126/Takali Wg	UK/Malta
E L Joyce	RNZAF	9/2/3	10/2/3	73 & 243 Wg	ME
A E Marshall	RAF	9/1/1	16+2sh/2/1	73	ME
R N Cullen	RAF	9/1/-	15/2/1	80	Greece
K W Driver	SAAF	9/-/-	10/-/-	1 SAAF & 274	EA/ME
G H Westlake	RAF	8+2sh/1/2	9+2sh/1/3	213 & 80	UK/Syria/ME
J Denis	FFAF	8.5/1/-	8.5/1/-	1 FF Flt/73/GC III/2 *Alsace*	ME
R R S Tuck	RAF	8/2/2	27+2sh/6/6.5	257 & Duxford Wg	UK
W J Storey	RAAF	8/2/-	8/2/-	135	UK/Burma
G E C Genders	RAF	7.5/2/4	8+2sh/3/3+2sh	33	Greece/NA
F A W J Wilson	RAF	7.5/1/3	8.5/2/5	80 & 213	Syria/ME
L Cottingham	RAF	7.5/1/-	11.5/1/-	33	Greece
R H Talbot	SAAF	7.5/-/3	9.5/-/3	274 & 1 SAAF	ME
J E Frost	SAAF	7.5/-/1	14+2sh/2+2sh/2+1sh	3 SAAF	EA
J A S Allen	RAF	7/3/6	7/3/6	232	FE
G R Tweedale	RAAF	7/2/2	7/2/2	43 & 126	UK/Malta
M S Osler	SAAF	7/-/2	9.5/-/2	1 SAAF	ME
F R Carey	RAF	7/-/1	25+3sh/3/8	43/245/135/267 Wg	UK/Burma
D G S Honor	RAF	6+3sh/-/1+2sh	6+3sh/-/1+3sh	274 & 258 Wg	ME/Greece
R A Barton	RAF	6+2sh/1/1	15+5sh/2/5+4sh	249	UK/Malta
J T Shaw	RAF	6.5/2/2	6.5/2/2	3 & 32	UK/NA
G J King	RAF	6.5/-/2	6.5/-/2	232 & 242	FE
T F Dalton-Morgan	RAF	6.5/-/-	14+3sh/1/4	43	UK
L R S Waugh	SAAF	6/2/3	6/2/4	1 SAAF	ME
R L Dovell	RAF	6/2/-	6/2/-	17 & 232	UK/FE
R R H Bowes	RAAF	6.5/-/2	6.5/-/2	79	Burma
H T Nicholls	RAF	6/1/3	6/1/3	232	FE
E M Taylor	RAF	6/1/-	6/1/-	136 & 232	UK/FE
C E Hamilton	RAF	6/-/-	6/-/-	261 & 185	Malta
G E Horricks	RCAF	5+2sh/0.5/6	7+2sh/0.5/6	185	Malta
J A Sowrey	RAF	5+2sh/-/1	5+2sh/-/1	605/73/213/80	UK/ME
D U Barnwell	RAF	5+2sh/-/-	5+2sh/-/-	185 & MNFU	Malta
J F Pain	RAF	5.5/7/5	7.5/10/6	261 & 73	Malta/ME
J L Boyd	RAAF	5.5/4/10	5+2sh/5/11	135/242/185	UK/Malta
R G Foskett	RAAF	5.5/-/3	6.5/-/5	80 & 94	ME

Name	Service/ Nationality	Kills 1941-45	Total Kills	Sqn/s	Theatre/s
B J Parker	RAF	5/4/4	5/4/4	232 & 242	UK/FE
I Julian	RNZAF	5/2/3	5/2/3	232 & 232	FE
S R Peacock-Edwards	RAF	5/1/1	6.5/1/4	261/258/30	Malta/Ceylon
F Mason	RAF	5/1/1	5/1/1	80	ME
J M V Carpenter	RAF	5/-/2	8/1/3	46 & 126	Malta
H P Lardner-Burke	RAF	5/-/2	7.5/-/3	126	Malta
J F Barrick	RCAF	5/-/2	5/-/2	17	Burma
R E P Brooker	RAF	5/-/1	8/2/1	1/232/242	UK/FE
J D Dygryn	Czech	5/-/1	5/-/1	1	UK
A Littolf	FFAF	5/-/1	6+8sh/0.5/1	73 & 274	ME
J-F Demozay	FFAF	5/-/-	18/2/4	1 & 242	UK
P R St Quentin	RAF	5/-/-	9/1/1	33	ME
T P M Cooper-Slipper	RAF	5/-/-	8+4sh/-/4	135 & 232	UK/FE
J R Perrin	RAAF	5/-/-	6/1/-	3 RAAF	ME
D R Beard	RAF	5/-/-	5/-/-	73	ME
A J Botha	SAAF	5/-/-	5/-/-	1 SAAF	ME
R Dahl	RAF	5/-/-	5/-/-	80	Greece/Syria
S vB Theron	SAAF	5/-/-	5/-/-	3 SAAF	EA
A J Rippon	RAF	4+3sh/-/0.5	4+3sh/-/0.5	261	Malta
G E Goodman	RAF	4+2sh/-/-	10+6sh/-/2.5	73	NA
W A G Conrad	RCAF	4.5/3/8	5+3sh/3/10+2sh	274	ME
A J Hancock	RAF	4.5/3/-	5+2sh/3/2	80 & 213	Syria/UK/ME
H W Ayre	RAF	4.5/2/-	4.5/2/-	261	Malta
S Linnard	RAF	4.5/1/3	6.5/3/5	274	ME
R J Cork	RN	4.5/1/1	9+2sh/1/4	880	Med/Madagascar
R A Brabner	RN	4.5/1/0.5	5.5/1/0.5	801	Med
O O Ormrod	RAF	2+4sh/2/-	2+4sh/2/-	605 & 185	UK/Malta
H A Armstrong	RAF	2+3sh/1/-	2+3sh/1/-	135	Burma
G C C Palliser	RAF	1+5sh/2sh/1	4+7sh/2sh/3	249	UK/Malta

Notes

Multiple shared claims are shown i.e. '+3sh' which indicates three half/part shares in addition to any full claims

Theatre abbreviations:

UK - UK and Europe
NA - North Africa
NG - New Guinea
EA - East Africa
FE - Singapore and the East Indies
Med - Mediterranean
ME - Middle East
Rus - Russia & Arctic
Burma - India and Burma

Other theatres are given in full

Aces with some Hurricane claims

Name	Service/ Nationality	Kills 1941-45	Total Kills	Sqn/s	Theatre/s
R A Acworth	RAF	3/-/-	7/1/2	80 att	Greece
N leC Agazarian	RAF	1/-/-	5+3sh/-/4.5	274	ME
W S Arthur	RAAF	1/-/-	8/2/6	3 RAAF	ME
P V Ayerst	RAF	1/-/2	3+2sh/1/3	33 & 238	ME
D R S Bader	RAF	0.5/-/-	20+4sh/6.5/ 11	242	UK
I J Badger	RAF	2/-/-	4?/4/5	87/73/94	UK/ME
C S Bamberger	RAF	2/-/-	5/1/2	261 & 185	Malta
R G A Barclay	RAF	2/-/-	6+2sh/6/4	238	ME
R E Bary	RAF	1/-/1	2+4sh/2/2	229/274/80	UK/ME
A W A Bayne	RAF	1/1/-	7+4sh/2+4sh/2	30 & 136	Ceylon/Burma
F V Beamish	RAF	1/-/-	10/11.5/5	N/Weald Wg	UK
R P Beamont	RAF	-/-/1	9.5/2/4	87 & 79	UK
H J S Beazley	RAF	-/2.5/2sh	2+4sh/3.5/ 2.5	249	UK/Malta
K H Blair	RAF	-/1/-	6+2sh/5.5/3	151 & 1453 Flt	UK
H P Blatchford	RAF	1/1/-	5+3sh/4/4.5	257	UK
B J L Boyle	SAAF	2.5/-/-	5.5/-/-	1 SAAF	EA
B A Bretherton	RAAF	2/-/-	8/-/-	73	NA
C E Broad	RAF	0.5/-/2	2.5?/2/5	185	Malta
J M Bruen	RN	3.5/-/-	4+4sh/-/2+2sh	800 & RNFS	*Indomitable/Biter/*ME
S Brzeski	Pole	1+2sh/-/-	7+3sh/4/1	249 & 317	UK
G Burges	RAF	3/-/3	7/2/6	261	Malta
C R Bush	RAF	-/1/-	3.5?/2/3	258	UK
C E Casbolt	RAF	4/-/1	13.5/1/3.5	80	Greece
N Castelain	FFAF	0.5/-/-	4+3sh/-/-	1 FF Flt/73	ME
P N Charlton	RN	3/2/1	3+3sh/2/1	803	ME
W L Chisholm	RCAF	-/1/1	6+2sh/4/4	80 att	ME
D G Clift	RAF	-/1/-	3+2sh/2/-	79 & MSFU	UK/Atlantic
A C Cochrane	RAF	1/-/-	4+2/1/2	87	UK/NA
R J P Collingwood	SAAF	4/1/1	5/1/1	1 SAAF	ME
B G Collyns	RAF	1/-/-	5+2sh/1/3	238 & 1	UK
A G Conway	RAF	3/-1	7/1/4	136	Burma
R W Cross	RAF	3/1/6	9/1/3	136	Burma
R M Crosley	RN	3.5/1/-	4.5/1/-	813/800/804	*Eagle/Biter/Dasher*
D Crowley-Milling	RAF	0.5/-/1.5	4.5/1.5/3.5	242 & 181	UK
R T P Davidson	RAF	3/1/2	4+2sh/2/2	30 & 261	ME/Ceylon
G A Daymond	US	3/-/-	7/-/1	71	UK
E H Dean	RAF	5/-/-	5/-/-	33 & 274	ME
W G Dodd	RAF	-/2/2	6+2sh/3/4	185	Malta
B Drake	RAF	1/-/-	20+2/4+2/7	128	WA
A Duncan	SAAF	2/-/-	4.5/1/-	1 SAAF	EA
P H Dunn	RAF	1/-/-	6+3sh/2/1.1	274	ME
W R Dunn	US	3/0.5/-	9/1.5/-	71	UK
P W Dunning-White	RAF	1.5/-/-	3+2sh/2.5/1	145 & 615	UK
B Duperier	FFAF	1/-/1	5+2sh/1/3.5	242 & 615	UK
W G Eagle	RAF	2/1/3	7/1/3	274	ME
D F K Edghill	RAF	4/-/1	7/-/1	229	ME
S R Edner	US	/0.5/-	5/0.5/1	121	UK
H W Eliot	RAF	1/1/-	8.5/1.5/1	261	Malta
R V Ellis	RAF	3/-/-	3+4sh/-/1	73	ME
T A F Elsdon	RAF	-/-/2	8/-/2	257 & 136	UK/Burma
H J Everard	RCAF	1/1/-	5.5/3/3	17	Burma
J P Falkowski	Pole	1/-/-	9/1/-	32 & 315	UK

Name	Service/ Nationality	Kills 1941-45	Total Kills	Sqn/s	Theatre/s
P C P Farnes	RAF	-/-/5	7+2sh/2/11	229	Malta
J M Faure	SAAF	3/1/-	5.5/1/1	1 SAAF	ME
L S Ford	RCAF	-/-/0.5	6/-/2.5	402	UK
R W Foster	RAF	-/-/1	6.5/3/6.5	605	UK
C H Fry	RAF	1/-/-	5/2/1	112	Greece
D Fulford	RAF	2/-/-	4+2sh/1/-	261	Ceylon
A K Gabszewicz	Pole	2sh/-/-	8+3/1.5/2	316	UK
G W Garton	RAF	2.5/-/-	7+3sh/2/2	73 & 3 RAAF att	ME
G H Gaynor	SAAF	2/-/3	5.5/-/6	1 SAAF	ME
J Gillies	RAF	2/-/-	5.5/1.5/2	615/136/79	Burma
I R Gleed	RAF	1.5/1/-	13+3sh/4+ 3sh/4	87	UK
N V Glew	RAF	1/-/1	3+3sh/2/6	260	ME
G Godden	RAF	4/-/1	7/-/1	274	ME
A P Goldsmith	RAAF	1/-/-	16.5/2/7	126	Malta
W A Goold	RAAF	1/-/-	5/1/5	607	Burma
D C Gordon	RCAF	2/2/2	9+2sh/5/5	274	ME
D L Gould	RAF	3?/5/-	5/5/-	213/274/33	UK/ME
E J Gracie	RAF	-/-/1	7+3sh/5/6	601 & 126	UK/Malta
R D Grassick	RAF	2/3/1	7.5/3/2	242 & 260	UK/ME
C F Gray	RAF	0.5/-/-	27+2sh/7+ 4sh/12	1	UK
R A Haggar	RAF	1/-/-	7/1/3	56	UK
R F Hamlyn	RAF	2/-/-	10.5/1/1	242	UK
O V Hanbury	RAF	1/-/-	10+2sh/1+3sh/6	260	ME
P R Hanks	RAF	1/1/-	11+4sh/1+ 3sh/6	56 & 257	UK
C Haw	RAF	3/-/2	4?/-/1.5	504 & 81	UK/Russ
G D L Haysom	RAF	1/-/0.5	5/1/1.5	79	UK
J C F Hayter	RNZAF	2/1/-	5/1/3	605/33/274/74	UK/ME/Iran
J B Hobbs	RAF	2/-/-	4+3sh/-/-	274	ME
R H Holland	RAF	-/1/-	5.5/4/6.5	615 & 607	Burma
F Holman	RAF	2.5/-/-	8.5?/-/-	33	Greece
A U Houle	RCAF	3.5/1/3	11.5/1/7	213	ME
P H Hugo	RAF	0.5/-/-	17.5/3/7	615	UK
A H Humphrey	RAF	2/2/-	7/2/-	175 & 6	UK/ME
R J Hyde	RAF	2/1/1	5/1/1	261	Malta
J F Jackson	RAAF	4/1/-	7/1/-	3 RAAF	ME
P Jeffrey	RAAF	1.5//-/-	5.5/-/1	3 RAAF	ME
C G StD Jeffries	RAF	2.5/2/2	3+3sh/3/2	261 & 185	Malta
J Jeka	Pole	1/-/-	8/-/4	306	UK
G R A McG Johnson	RAF	4/2/1	9+2sh/2/2	73	ME
H A S Johnston	RAF	1/-/0.5	5.5/5/2.5	257 & 133	UK
M E Jowsey	RCAF	-/-/0.5	5/1/3	33	ME
M T Judd	RAF	-/-/1	5?/-/3	238 & 33	ME
G C Keefer	RCAF	4/1/6	12/2/9	274	ME
J A Kent	RAF	-/-/1	12/3/2	17 Sector	NA
G V W Kettlewell	RAF	2/-/-	5/1/-	80 & 213	Greece/ME
B Kratkoruky	Czech	2/-/-	2+3sh/1/-	1	UK
J B Kremski	Pole	0.5/-/-	3+4sh/1/5	308	UK
W S Krol	Pole	1.5/-/-	8+1sh/1/0.5	302	UK
O Kucera	Czech	2/1/1	5+2sh/1/1	111 & 312	UK
J Latimer	RAF	-/1/1	7+2sh/1/1.5	310 & 1455 Flt	UK
C J Laubscher	SAAF	2.5/-/-	4+2/2/3	274 & 261	ME/Malta/Iran
K A Lawrence	RAF	2.5/-/3	4+2/-/9.5	185	Malta
P W Lefevre	RAF	3/-/1	5+5sh/0.5/1	46 & 126	Malta
D A R G Leroy du Vivier	Belg	2+2sh/-/-	3+2sh/-/1	43	UK

Name	Service/ Nationality	Kills 1941-45	Total Kills	Sqn/s	Theatre/s
G J LeMesurier	SAAF	2/1/-	3?/1/1	1 SAAF	EA, ME
D H Loftus	SAAF	1.5/-/-	4.5/-/3	1 & 2 SAAF	EA/ME
M M Maciejowski	Pol	2/-/-	10.5/1/1	249	UK
K W Mackenzie	RAF	2/-/-	10+3/2/1	247	UK
J F Mackie	RAF	1/-/-	7/-/-	33	Greece
W I H Maguire	RAF	1/-/-	13/1/2	253	UK
J M Maridor	FFAF	0.5/-/-	3.5?/2/3	615	UK
R G Marland	RAF	-/1/-	5+2sh/4/3.5	229	ME
R Marples	RAF	0.5/1/-	2+5/4/3	127 & 238	ME
R F Martin	RAF	1.5/-/-	5+3sh/-/1	73	ME
W H Martyn	RN	1.5/-/-	2+3sh/-/-	800	*Indomitable*
P G H Matthews	RAF	-/-/1	6+3sh/2/4.5	73 att	ME
H C Mayers	RAF	0.5/-/2	11.5/3.5/6	601 & 94	UK
D A S McKay	RAF	-/-/1	15/-/5	213/33/274	ME
D A P McMullen	RAF	-/1/-	17+5/6.5/12	151	UK
P E Meagher	RAF	2/-/-	9/2/-	?	UK
H O Mehre	Nor	1/-/2	6/-/10	242 & 331	UK
P C R Metlerkamp	SAAF	4/-/2	5/-/4	1 SAAF	ME
J M Morgan	RAF	2/-/3	7.5/0.5/8	80	ME
E J Morris	RAF	0.5/-/-	2+5/1/3	238/250/274	UK/ME
T C Morris	RAF	1/-/-	3+2/-/3sh	274	ME
E B Mortimer-Rose	RAF	3.5/-/3sh	9+4sh/3+2sh/5+6sh	249 & 185	Malta
P W O Mould	RAF	1/-/2	8+3sh/-/5	261 & 185	Malta
J W Neil	RAF	3/2/6	5/3/6	274	ME
T F Neil	RAF	1/-/-	12+4sh/2/1	249	UK/Malta
P A Newton	RAF	3/2/3	5?/2/3	33	Greece
S C Norris	RAF	1/-/2sh	8.5/1/1+3sh	126 & 33	Malta/ME
E Nowakiewicz	Pol	1/-/0.5	4+2sh/1/2sh	302	UK
P Olver	RAF	1/2/3	4+2sh/3+1sh/4+2sh	238 & 213	ME
J A O'Neil	RAF	1/-/-	?	601/238/176	UK/ME/India
N Orton	RAF	-/1/-	17/8/3+5sh	242	UK
R Pare	SAAF	4/-/-	5/-/.5	1 SAAF	EA
T L Patterson	RAF	2/-/1	7/1/1	274	ME
T G Paxton	RAAF	4/-/-	5.5/-/-	30	ME/Ceylon
M G F Pedley	RAF	2/-/2	3+2sh/-/3	323 Wg	NA
C O J Pegge	RAF	2/-/-	8/1/3	127	ME
C G Peterson	US	1/-/-	8/3/6	71	UK
P R P Powell	RAF	-/1/-	7+2sh/3/4	121	UK
G F Powell-Sheddan	RAF	1/2sh/-	4+2sh/2sh/-	258/615/MNFU	UK/Malta
J Prihoda	Czech	1.5/2/1	4.5/3/2	1	UK
A C Rawlinson	RAAF	3/-/1	8/2/8	3 RAAF	ME
B Ritchie	RN	3.5/-/-	5+2sh/-/-	800	*Indomitable/Biter*
G D Robertson	RCAF	-/1/1	4.5/1/4.5	402	UK
M E S Robinson	SAAF	0.5/-/-	5.5/1/1	1 SAAF	ME
M Rook	RAF	1.5/1/2	3.5?/1/2	504/81/43	UK/Rus/NA
J K Ross	RAF	0.5/-/-	2+5sh/2/-	17 & 134	UK/Rus
K Rutkowski	Pol	-/-/1	5.5/2/1	306	UK
C J Samouelle	RAF	1/-/2	10.5/4/11	80	ME
W A J Satchell	RAF	3/2/12.5	7/5/12.5	302/Takali Wg	UK/Malta
J H W Saunders	RAAF	3/-/2	6/-/2	3 RAAF	ME
D J Scott	RNZAF	3.5/4/4	5+3sh/4+ 2sh/5.5	3	UK
J B Selby	RAF	4/-/-	5/-/-	73	ME
J W C Simpson	RAF	3/-/-	9.5/1/1	245	UK
I S Smith	RAF	-/1/-	8/1/4	151	UK

Name	Service/ Nationality	Kills 1941-45	Total Kills	Sqn/s	Theatre/s
J D Smith	RAF	2/-/1	7.5/1/2	73	ME
W A Smith	RAF	4/2/2	5/3/7+3sh	229	ME
F J Soper	RAF	2/-/1.5	10+4sh/-/2.5	257	UK
K Sporny	Pol	-/1/-	5/1/1	302	UK
L Srom	Czech	-/0.5/-	4+2sh/2.5/2	245	UK
H J Starrett	RAF	4sh/1/-	3+4sh/2/-	33	Greece
G H Steege	RAAF	4/-/3	8/2/5	3 RAAF	ME
J Stehlik	Czech	0.5/1/1	3+7sh/1.5/1	312	UK
M M Stephens	RAF	1/-/-	15+3sh/1/5	274/80/Turk AF	ME
C A C Stone	RAF	2/-/2	5+2sh/-/2	607/17/135	UK/Burma
D W A Stones	RAF	1+2sh/1/1+2	7+5sh/4.5/4+2sh	79/249/MNFU/605/67	UK/Malta/Burma
J A S Storrar	RAF	2/-/1	12+2sh/2.5/3	73 & 1697 Flt	ME/UK
F Surma	Pol	-/0.5/-	5/3/1	242 & 308	UK
F B Sutton	RAF	1/3/-	4.5/2/1	136 & 135	Burma
H N Sweetman	RNZAF	0.5/-/-	1+2?sh/1.5/ 2.5	486	UK
H Szczesny	Pol	2sh/-/-	8+3sh/-/1	317	UK
H N Tamblyn	RAF	-/-/1	5.5/1/2	242	UK
F F Taylor	RAF	3/1/-	7/2/1	261	Malta
N Taylor	RAF	4/-/2	7/1/2	601 & MSFU	UK/Atlantic
P D Thompson	RAF	1+3sh/2/-	1+3sh (6?)/2/3	605/261/185	UK/Malta
P W Townsend	RAF	1/-/-	9+2sh/2/4	85	UK
O V Tracey	RAF	3/-/-	6/3/1	274	ME
W P F Treacy	RAF	0.5/1/-	1+3sh/1/-	242	UK
R W Turkington	RAF	1/-/-	9+3/1/4	43	UK/NA
P StG B Turnbull	RAAF	4/-/-	12/1/2	3 RAAF	ME
P S Turner	RAF	0.5/-/-	10.5/1/8	242/249/134	UK/Malta/ME
J R Urwin-Mann	RAF	-/-/1	8+2sh/2/3	238 & 80	UK/ME
D C Usher	RAF	1/-/-	5/-/2	213	ME
C A van Vliet	SAAF	3/-/-	4?/-/-	1 SAAF	ME
A Vasatko	Czech	-/1/1	4+10/2+2sh	312	UK
V B S Verity	RAF	-/1/-	8.5/3/4.5	96	UK
A D Wagner	RAF	2/-/1	9/-/5	151 & 30	UK/ME/Ceylon
D R Walker	RAF	3.5/-/0.5	4.5/-/2.5	30/260/127	ME
J A Walker	RAF	-/0.5/1	6.5/0.5/1	111/94	UK/ME
J E Walker	RCAF	1/1/-	9.5/4/12+3sh	81	Russia
D H Ward	RAF	4/1/1	6.5/1/4	87 & 73	UK/ME
J L Waters	RAF	1/-/1	5?/-/1	261	Malta
J H Wedgewood	RAF	1/-/1	10/-/12	80 att	ME
R West	RAF	-/-/2	8/3/8.5	43 & 126	UK/Malta
I B Westmacott	RAF	1/2/-	3+2sh/2/2	56/261/185/ MNFU/1435 Flt	UK/Malta
J H Whalen	RCAF	3/-/-	6/-/1	30/17/261/34	Ceylon/Burma
P R W Wickham	RAF	3/-/-	10/7/15	33	Greece
G A Williams	RNZAF	1.5/-/-	3.5?/2/4	67	Burma
L A Wilmot	SAAF	2.5/-/-	4.5/-/-	1 SAAF	EA/ME
A F Wilson	RAF	1/-/-	4.5/1/3	103 MU	ME
S Witorzenc	Pol	1/-/-	5.5/-/2	306 & 302	UK
H deC A Woodhouse	RAF	1/-/-	3+2sh/-/4	71 & OC Ftr Force	UK/Burma
W J Woods	RAF	1/2/-	6.5/2/1	261 & 80	Malta/Greece
E W Wright	RAF	-/-/3	3+3sh/3/8.5	605/232	UK/FE
P G Wykeham-Barnes	RAF	4/1/-	14+3sh/1/2+2sh	274/73/257	ME/UK
J W Yarra	RAAF	-/1/-	12/2/6	126/229/185	Malta/ME
J N Yates	RAF	1.5/1/2	4.5?/2/2	607	UK/Burma
M H Young	RAF	1/-/3	7+6sh/-/3	1422 Flt/73/213	UK/ME

1

Hurricane IIC BE581/JX-E of Flt Lt K M Kuttelwascher, No 1(F) Sqn, Tangmere, April-June 1942

One of the most successful of the RAF's night intruder pilots was the Czech Karel Kuttelwascher, who claimed all his RAF victories flying Hurricanes with No 1 Sqn. Although he became an ace with the unit in June 1941, he really came to prominence for his night intruder sorties. Between 1 April and 1 July 1942, he shot down 15 Luftwaffe bombers at, or near, their French bases flying this Hurricane IIC, which was painted black overall, and is seen with his total number of victory markings displayed in early 1942.

2

Hurricane IIB BE171/YB-B of Sgt J F Barrick, Mingaladon, No 17 Sqn, Burma, February 1942

An American who joined the RCAF, 'Tex' Barrick moved with No 17 Sqn to Burma after the Japanese invasion. He served throughout the long retreat, and claimed all his five victories during this period. The first two were scored flying this aircraft when, in a combat over Rangoon on 7 February 1942, he shot down two Ki-27 'Nate' fighters and damaged a third. This particular machine was assigned to No 17 Sqn's CO, Sqn Ldr 'Bunny' Stone DFC, but as fighters were scarce they were flown by any available pilots. It was one of the few desert camouflaged Hurricanes to reach Burma.

3

Hurricane IIB BG827/RS-W of Plt Off J H Whalen, No 30 Sqn, Ratmalana, Ceylon, April 1942

No 30 Sqn was flown off the carrier HMS *Indomitable* in early March 1942 to participate in the defence of Ceylon. One of its pilots was Canadian Jimmy Whalen who, on Easter Day 1942, flew this aircraft against Japanese carrier aircraft striking Colombo. The defenders were outnumbered, but Whalen was credited with three D3A 'Val' dive-bombers destroyed to become an ace, although these were his final air combat claims.

4

Hurricane IIC BP588/RS-X of Sqn Ldr S C Norris, No 33 Sqn, Benina, Libya, November-December 1942

By 1942 No 33 Sqn's aircraft wore the code letters RS, usually applied in a dark colour. This Hurricane was first used by the unit on 2 November 1942, and it soon became the CO's aircraft. Sqn Ldr Stan Norris, who had 8.5 victories, arrived that month, and flew BP588 on his first operation with No 33 on the 22nd, when he led six Hurricanes on a Hudson escort to Msus. The aircraft carries his rank pennant, and he flew it regularly until he left the squadron in February 1943.

5

Hurricane IIC BN230/FT-A of Sqn Ldr D A R G L Du Vivier, No 43 Sqn, Acklington, 25 April 1942

A Belgian who escaped to fly with the RAF, Leroy Du Vivier served exclusively with the RAF, and became the first Belgian to command an RAF squadron when, in January 1942, he took over No 43. He made his fifth, and last, claim flying this aircraft when he destroyed a Ju 88 over the North Sea on 25 April 1942, although he was also hit and wounded. The aircraft displays his various affiliations – the RAF Ensign, Belgian flag and No 43 Sqn's black and white checks.

6

Hurricane I V7101 of Flt Lt G Burges DFC, No 69 Sqn, Luqa, Malta, May 1941

George Burges was a founder member of the Gladiator Fighter Flight at Hal Far, and claimed seven victories, becoming an ace while flying a Hurricane on 18 January 1941. Later that month he reverted to his primary role with No 69 Sqn flying reconnaissance Marylands. No 69 Sqn received this Hurricane for flying against more dangerous targets, the fighter being lightened and fitted with two cameras. It was also repainted overall PR blue, and Burges flew it regularly until he left Malta on 6 June.

7

Hurricane IIB Z3781/XR-T of Plt Off W R Dunn, No 71 'Eagle' Sqn, North Weald, July 1941

Bill Dunn was the first American to 'make ace' in World War 2, a distinction he achieved flying with No 71 'Eagle' Sqn during the summer of 1941. His first three victories were scored with Hurricanes, the first two on 2 and 21 July in this aircraft, which carries the unit's caricature eagle badge on its nose. His final two victories, which made him an ace, came on 27 August shortly after the squadron converted to Spitfires.

8

Hurricane I V7562/TP-A of Sgt A E Marshall, No 73 Sqn, Sidi Haneish, Egypt, 5 January 1941

Alfred Marshall regarded this as his favourite Hurricane, and he made his first claim while flying it on 5 January when he shot down an SM.79 to achieve his eighth victory. The following day V7562 was used by fellow ace Jas Storrar to destroy a CR.42. It was not until 9 April that Marshall again claimed while flying this Hurricane, downing a Ju 52/3m transport over Derna and then sharing in the destruction of six Bf 110s found on the ground nearby.

9

Hurricane IIB Z3745/NV-B of Sqn Ldr G D L Haysom, No 79 Sqn, Fairwood Common, August 1941

South African David Haysom served with No 79 Sqn throughout the Battle of Britain, claiming four victories. A flight commander by April 1941, he shot down an He 111 to become an ace on the 1st of that month. In June Haysom assumed command of the squadron, his aircraft wearing the title *Fort St George, Madras Presidency* to display the squadron's wartime affiliation with this Indian state.

10

Hurricane I V7795 of Plt Off W Vale, No 80 Sqn, Eleusis, Greece and Maleme, Crete, April-May 1941

Possibly the most successful Hurricane of the Greek campaign, V7795 was delivered to No 80 Sqn on 9 April, and was extensively used by Bill Vale. There was no time to apply unit markings, and it flew as depicted. Vale was at the controls of this aircraft on 14 April, escorting Blenheim bombers over Bulgaria, when he shot down a Stuka – the following day he destroyed two Ju 88s. He also flew V7795 over Crete, where he claimed three Ju 88s, one Bf 109 and a Ju 87 destroyed. Vale was evacuated, but V7795 was abandoned on Crete.

11

Hurricane IIB Z4018/FH-41 of Flt Sgt C Haw, No 81 Sqn, Vaenga, Russia, September 1941

The leading pilot of the RAF expedition to north Russia during the autumn of 1941 was Flt Sgt 'Wag' Haw. On the afternoon of 12 September, he was flying this aircraft west of Murmansk when he gained the RAF's first victory in Russia. Haw destroyed a second Bf 109 in another aircraft some days later, but was flying Z4018 again on the 27th when he downed his third Messerschmitt fighter in the Arctic.

12

Hurricane I P3149/LK-P of Plt Off I J Badger, No 87 Sqn, St Mary's, Isles of Scilly, June-July 1941

To counter Luftwaffe reconnaissance flights over the UK's south-west approaches, 'B' Flight of No 87 Sqn was detached to the tiny airstrip at St Mary's in the Scilly Isles on 19 May 1941. Immediately after arrival, Ivor Badger was scrambled to the south-west to shoot down an Ar 196 seaplane, thus gaining his second victory. He returned to the islands on further detachments throughout the summer, when he regularly flew this aircraft, as did Sqn Ldr 'Widge' Gleed and Flg Off 'Bee' Beamont.

13

Hurricane IIB Z3427/AV-R of Plt Off S R Edner, No 121 'Eagle' Sqn, Kirton-in-Lindsay, 8 August 1941

Sel Edner joined the second 'Eagle' squadron soon after it was formed. On becoming operational, the unit was tasked with convoy patrols off the east coast, and during one on 8 August, some 50 miles off Hull, Edner and Sgt Jack Mooney attacked a Ju 88. They continued firing at it until their ammunition was exhausted, and the Junkers was last seen low over the sea, pouring smoke. No 121 Sqn's first combat therefore resulted in a probable claim.

14

Hurricane IIB BD776/WG-F of Sqn Ldr J I Kilmartin, No 128 Sqn, Hastings, Sierra Leone, 3 April 1942

No 128 was formed at Hastings, near Freetown, to defend the vital port against Vichy French aircraft based in Senegal. The CO, Sqn Ldr John 'Iggy' Kilmartin, who had 12 victories, flew this aircraft on a scramble on 3 April. It was usually flown by Sgt Arthur Todd, who had previously shot down a Vichy Martin 167. The aircraft wears No 128 Sqn's little-used code letters, together with a brightly coloured spinner.

15

Hurricane IIB Z5659/WK-C of Plt Off W J Storey, No 135 Sqn, Mingaladon, Burma, February 1942

On 6 February 1942 the Japanese attacked Mingaladon airfield, outside Rangoon, and Jack Storey scrambled in this

aircraft, leading six others aloft. Three Ki-27 'Nate' fighters of the 77th *Sentai* jumped them, and in the subsequent fight Storey shot down two and claimed two probables. He was again flying Z5659 on 23 February when he sent a 'Nate' into the jungle in flames for his fourth victory.

16

Hurricane IIB AP894/C of Flt Lt W J Storey, No 135 Sqn, 'George' and 'Hove' LGs, East Bengal, March-May 1943

On 5 March 1943 Jack Storey scrambled in this aircraft with 'A' Flight against hostile aircraft over the enemy port of Akyab. After a lengthy tail chase, he sent a 64th *Sentai* 'Oscar' into the sea to become an ace. After refuelling and rearming, Storey led his flight back to Akyab, where they encountered further 'Oscars', and he destroyed two more. It was also in AP894, which wore interim markings with the red removed from the fuselage roundel, that Storey claimed his eighth, and final, kill on 5 May.

17

Hurricane IIB BE198/HM-R of Plt Off A G Conway, No 136 Sqn, Red Road, Calcutta, India 10 July 1942

This aircraft was recorded in Plt Off Gordon Conway's log book as the one he was handling on 10 July 1942 when No 136 Sqn was based on the Red Road, in the centre of Calcutta. While taxying for take-off the starboard tyre punctured and Conway hit a stone balustrade. He destroyed three 'Oscars' flying Hurricanes, and later became an ace with the Spitfire.

18

Hurricane IIB BM913/N of Flt Lt E Brown, No 136 Sqn, Chittagong, East Bengal, May 1943

Eric 'Bojo' Brown was one of No 136 Sqn's leading pilots until his death in action in February 1944, by which time he had made five claims – four destroyed and one probable. He almost certainly used BM913 to shoot down a Ki-48 'Lily' in flames near Chittagong on 22 May 1943, this being his final Hurricane victory. The aircraft wears an interesting mix of markings, with the yellow-outlined fuselage roundel being much reduced and lacking the red centre. It also displays No 136 Sqn's woodpecker badge on the nose.

19

Hurricane I V6931/DZ-D of Flt Lt I S Smith, No 151 Sqn, Wittering, 10 May 1941

'Blackie' Smith was a flight commander with No 151 Sqn when it switched to nightfighting. He flew this aircraft for the first half of 1941, and probably used it to destroy an He 111 over London on the night of 10/11 May 1941. A Kiwi, Smith decorated the nose of his fighter with a New Zealand fern leaf. This aircraft was also flown by several of the squadron's other notable pilots, including Sgt Alan Wagner.

20

Hurricane IIB Z2961/K of Sgt G E Horricks, No 185 Sqn, Takali, Malta, 23 March 1942

Canadian Garth Horricks claimed regularly during early 1942, and he was regarded as one of the island's best pilots during this period. On 23 March, while flying this aircraft, he shared a Ju 88, which was later confirmed by the Royal Navy as having crashed six miles south of Kalafrana Bay. He became an ace two days later, but was withdrawn and rested soon afterwards.

21

Hurricane I Z4223/V of Flg Off G H Westlake, No 213 Sqn, Nicosia, Cyprus, July-October 1941

In July 1941 a detachment of No 80 Sqn, to which No 213 Sqn pilots were attached, was sent to Nicosia. Among them was George Westlake, who on 18 July scrambled in this Hurricane against four Ju 88s flying low over Morphou Bay. He attacked one and the bomber disintegrated in a fireball, making Westlake an ace in spectacular fashion. No 213 then became responsible for the defence of Cyprus, and on 26 August Westlake was airborne again in Z4223 when he caught a Cant Z1007. His first burst blew off the starboard aileron, causing the bomber to crash.

22

Hurricane IIC BE643/AK-U of Plt Off A U Houle, No 213 Sqn, Edku, Egypt, April 1942

Canadian Bert Houle flew this Hurricane IIC when No 213 Sqn was defending the port of Alexandria in the spring of 1942, but on one occasion he misjudged his approach in BE643 and sheared the fighter's undercarriage off. During this period No 213's aircraft had a hornet motif superimposed over the fuselage roundel. Each hornet was different, and they were applied by squadron pilot Sgt Wally Lack.

23

Hurricane IIB BE206/O of Flt Lt E W Wright, No 232 Sqn, Kallang, Singapore, 5 February 1942

'Ricky' Wright was one of No 232 Sqn's flight commanders. Having scrambled in this aircraft, he was hit and, while attempting a landing, crashed through a fence before stopping in a ditch. BE206 was the CO's aircraft, the fighter carrying his rank pennant and the unit's Dragon Ship badge near the cockpit. Wright became the squadron CO soon afterwards, but with the fall of Java he was captured, and spent the rest of the war as a PoW.

24

Hurricane I W9200/DX-? of Sqn Ldr J W C Simpson, No 245 Sqn, Aldergrove, Northern Ireland, 6 May 1941

John Simpson became CO of No 245 Sqn in December 1940, and his unit was tasked with countering enemy intrusions over the Irish Sea. W9200 was his assigned aircraft, and it wore a '?' in place of a letter and personal markings, along with an impressive scoreboard. Simpson was flying this aircraft on the night of 7 April when he destroyed an He 111 of III./KG 26. On the night of 5 May he brought down another to score his 12th victory, as indicated by the score displayed.

25

Hurricane I V7830 of Flg Off O V Tracey, No 274 Sqn, Gerawla, Egypt, 29 May 1941

Soon after Owen Tracey joined it, No 274 Sqn was involved in covering the Crete evacuation, and his destruction of a Ju 52/3m and a Bf 109 on 26 May made him an ace. Three days later he was flying this aircraft, decorated with No 274's lightning flash and spaghetti nose camouflage, over warships south of the island when he spotted Ju 88 '4U+EK' of 2(F)./123. Tracey duly sent it into the sea on fire to score his final victory.

26

Hurricane IIA DG631/NH-C of Flg Off W A G Conrad, No 274 Sqn, El Adem, Libya, 12 February 1942

On 8 February 1942 Flg Off Wally Conrad flew DG631 on an early patrol over Martuba. The Hurricanes were bounced, losing two of their number, although Conrad was able to claim a probable. Four days later he was again in this aircraft when a formation of I./StG 3 Ju 87s was encountered over Tobruk, and he was able to claim one destroyed and two damaged. Conrad became an ace in June of that year.

27

Hurricane IIB Z3437/DU-K of Sgt O Kucera, No 312 'Czech' Sqn, Kenley, July 1941

Otmar Kucera joined Czech-manned No 312 Sqn in the spring of 1941 and was allocated this aircraft, which he flew regularly. Returning in it from an escort mission on 18 June, he was attacked by three Bf 109s. Kucera fired two bursts at one, scoring hits on its port wing and canopy, but only claiming a probable. His scored his first confirmed victory while flying another aircraft.

28

Hurricane I V7339/JH-X of Sgt S Brzeski, No 317 'Wilenski' Sqn, Fairwood Common, 10 July 1941

Stanislaw Brzeski initially joined No 249 Sqn, but later moved to No 317 'Wilenski' Sqn, which flew sweeps over France, despite being based in South Wales. Escorting Blenheims on just such a mission on 10 July, Brzeski was flying this aircraft (the regular mount of Sgt Malinowski) when he encountered Bf 109s over Le Havre – he shared one destroyed with Flt Lt Szczesny. Brzeski's first Spitfire victory, in November, made him an ace.

29

Hurricane IIB BD734/FN-D of Sgt S Heglund, No 331 'Norwegian' Sqn, Skeabrae, Orkney, October-November 1941

No 331 Sqn was the first Norwegian-manned fighter unit to be established in the RAF, and it only briefly flew Hurricanes between July and November 1941. Among its first crop of pilots, several later became aces, including Svein Heglund, whose final total was 14.5 destroyed. He flew this aircraft on three occasions, although his regular Hurricane was BD863/FN-K. As well as a Norwegian flag, BD734 also displays the Nordic name Odin.

30

Hurricane IIB BD707/AE-C of Flt Sgt G D Robertson, No 402 Sqn RCAF, Southend, 18 September 1941

Flt Sgt Graham Robertson made claims for one aircraft damaged and another probably destroyed while flying the Hurricane. The latter claim was made on 18 September 1941, when Robertson flew this aircraft in combat with Bf 109s over the Channel. At the time No 402 Sqn was engaged in fighter-bomber attacks on targets in France and the Channel, which meant air combat claims were rare. Robertson subsequently became an ace flying Spitfires during the Normandy campaign.

31

Hurricane IIB BG713/UP-O of Plt Off O Ormrod, No 605 Sqn, Hal Far, Malta, December 1941-January 1942

One of the least-known aces of the Malta battles, Plt Off Oliver Ormrod arrived with No 605 Sqn in November 1941. On 27 December he helped mark out the codes on No 605 Sqn's aircraft, and BG713 became 'his', coded 'O' as his previous aircraft had been. Although he flew it regularly, he made no claims in the aircraft. Ormrod was killed in action on 22 April , by which time he had accumulated six victories (four of them shared). He was the last ace to die in a Hurricane over Malta.

32

Hurricane IIB BE332 of Plt Off J A Campbell, No 605 Sqn, Tjililitan, Java, 25 February 1942

'Red' Campbell was the most successful of the US 'Eagle' pilots sent to the Far East. They went initially as members of No 258 Sqn, the survivors of which became No 605 Sqn in Java. On 25 February Campbell flew BE332 to intercept an incoming raid, and he duly sent NAP 1/c Ide's Zero to its destruction to score his fourth victory. BE332 was hit, however, and part of the wing broke off. Campbell baled out, wounded, and became a PoW when Java fell.

33

Hurricane IIC Z3574(?)/OK-2, personal aircraft of the AOC Malta, Air Vice Marshal K R Park, Luqa, Malta, October-November 1942

One of the RAF's great fighter commanders, Air Vice Marshal Keith Park became an ace flying Bristol F2B Fighters during World War 1. On becoming AOC Malta in July 1942, he acquired his own aircraft, coded OK-2. Its precise identity is uncertain, but is believed to have been Z3574. Park regularly flew this aircraft on visits to his beleaguered airfields, most publicly at the opening of Krendi on 10 November 1942 when he performed a memorable beat-up of the airfield.

34

Sea Hurricane IA V6802/LU-B of Plt Off A S C Lumsden, Merchant Ship Fighter Unit, MV *Daghestan*, North Atlantic, September-October 1941

All MSFU pilots were volunteers, and Alec Lumsden served in SS *Daghestan* in the Atlantic under Capt Bobbin. He experienced no operational launches, but his Hurricat was launched near Anglesey at the end of each voyage. On 6 October 1941 weather forced him to land at Sealand. Lumsden had previously flown Spitfires with No 118 Sqn, and after the war he became well-known as an aviation writer.

35

Hurricane I V7772 of Flg Off A C Rawlinson, No 3 Sqn RAAF, Amriya, Egypt, February 1941

This Hurricane was flown by Alan Rawlinson at Amriya soon after it was delivered to the squadron. The fighter displays what was then the standard colour scheme, and it enjoyed considerable success when Rawlinson sent two Ju 87s down in flames near Tobruk on 3 April 1941 to score his first

confirmed victories. Two days later Flg Off John Jackson was flying this aircraft when he downed a Ju 87 for his fourth kill.

36

Hurricane I P3967/OS-B of Flt Lt J R Perrin, No 3 Sqn RAAF, Mararua, Libya, 5 April 1941

'Jock' Perrin was the only member of No 3 Sqn RAAF to became a Hurricane ace during the brief period the unit was equipped with the Hawker fighter. In the late afternoon of 5 April 1941, he took off in this aircraft from Mararua to cover retreating ground forces, and soon spotted a dozen unescorted Ju 87s of 4./StG 2 south of Barce. In the subsequent battle, Perrin shot down three to become an ace.

37

Hurricane IIB BG971/AX-V of Maj G J Le Mesurier, No 1 Sqn SAAF, LG 92, Egypt, 3 July 1942

3 July 1942 was a day of heavy air fighting, and in the evening 'Lemmie' Le Mesurier led No 1 Sqn to intercept a big Ju 87 raid on the El Alamein area. The squadron enjoyed great success, with Le Mesurier destroying the first Stuka, which exploded under his fire. The following evening, however, he was bounced by Bf 109s and brought down near El Imayid. His wounds caused him to be evacuated to South Africa.

38

Hurricane I 289/A of Capt J E Frost, No 3 Sqn SAAF, Jigigga, Abyssinia, March-April 1941

The leading SAAF ace of World War 2 was John Frost, who regularly flew Hurricane 289. He scored his first success while flying this aircraft on 29 March 1941, when he shot down a CR.42 near Diredawa. It was his sixth victory. Frost also destroyed several Italian aircraft on the ground during April in this Hurricane, and on the 30th claimed his eighth, and final, victory of the campaign when he attacked a low-flying SM. 79. After two attacks the crew baled out.

39

Sea Hurricane IB Z4550/G of Lt Cdr J M Bruen, 800 NAS, HMS *Indomitable*, Malta convoy, 12 August 1942

'Bill' Bruen commanded 800 NAS when it formed part of the escort to the vital *Pedestal* convoy heading for Malta. As heavy air attacks developed on 12 August, Bruen was launched in this aircraft against a Ju 88 attack. He downed one of the attackers, and two hours later, again in Z4550, he led his section against an Italian torpedo-bomber attack. Bruen shared in the destruction of an SM.84, before chasing an SM.79, which he shot down to 'make ace'.

40

Sea Hurricane IIB JS355 of Lt Cdr J M Bruen, 800 NAS, HMS *Biter*, Operation *Torch*, 8 November 1942

During Operation *Torch* 800 NAS's Sea Hurricane IIs had their roundels overpainted with US stars to make the operation appear an exclusively American one. Bruen led the escort for a dawn Albacore attack on La Seina airfield, Oran, but approaching the target the force was bounced by Vichy D.520 fighters. Bruen spotted a Dewoitine threatening an Albacore, and coming in high from astern, he hit the French fighter's engine, which burst into flames. The pilot baled out, giving Bruen his eighth, and last, victory.

BIBLIOGRAPHY

Baker, E C R, *Ace of Aces.* Crecy, 1992

Barker, Ralph, *The Hurricats.* Pelham, 1978

Brown, James Ambrose, *A Gathering of Eagles.* Purnell, 1970

Brown, James Ambrose, *Eagles Strike.* Purnell, 1975

Cotton, Sqn Ldr M C. *Hurricanes over Burma.* Grub St, 1995

Crosley, Cdr R M, *They Gave Me a Seafire.* Airlife, 1986

Cull, Brian, *249 at War.* Grub St, 1997

Donahue, Flt Lt A G, DFC, *Last Flight From Singapore.* Macmillan, 1944

Franks, Norman, *Hurricanes over the Arakan,* PSL, 1989

Gillison, Douglas, *RAAF 1939-1942* (Official History). AWM, 1962

Golley, John, *Hurricanes over Murmansk.* PSL, 1987

Griffin John and Kostenuk Samuel, *RCAF Squadron Histories and Aircraft.* Samuel Stevens, 1977

Halley, James, *Squadrons of the RAF and Commonwealth.* Air Britain, 1988

Halliday, Hugh, *Woody, A fighter Pilot's Album.* CANAV, 1987

Haughland, Verne, *The Eagle Squadrons.* David and Charles, 1979

Herrington, John, *Australia in the War 1939-45,* Series 3 Volume 3. Halstead Press, 1962

Holloway, Peter, *Desert Wings.* Melverley, 2002

Jefford, Wg Cdr C G, *RAF Squadrons.* Airlife, 1988 and 2001

Kelly, Terence, *Hurricane over the Jungle.* William Kimber, 1977

Listemann, Philippe, Tilley P-A and Eherengardt, C-J, *Les Pilotes de Chasse Francaise.* Aero Editions, 1999

Louw, Martin and Bouwer, Stephaan, *SAAF at War.* Chris van Rensburg Publications, 1995

Minterne, Don, *History of 73 Sqn,* Part 2. Tutor, 1997

Rawlings, John D R, *Fighter Squadrons of the RAF.* Macdonald, 1969

Richards, Denis, *RAF Official History 1939-45,* Part 2. HMSO, 1954

Shores, Christopher, *Aces High Vol 2.* Grub St, 1999

Shores, Christopher, *Dust Clouds over the Middle East.* Grub St, 1996

Shores, Christopher and Cull, Brian with Izawa, Yasuho, *Bloody Shambles* Vols 1 and 2. Grub St, 1992 and 1993

Shores, Christopher and Cull, Brian with Maliza, Nicola, *Malta - the Hurricane Years - 1940-41.* Grub St, 1987

Shores, Christopher and Cull, Brian with Maliza, Nicola, *Malta - the Spitfire Year - 1942.* Grub St, 1988

Shores, Christopher and Cull, Brian with Maliza, Nicola, *The Air Battle for Yugoslavia, Greece and Crete.* Grub St, 1987

Shores, Christopher and Ring, Hans, *Fighters over the Desert.* Neville Spearman, 1969

Shores, Christopher and Williams Clive, *Aces High* Vol 1. Grub St, 1994

Shores, Christopher, Ring, Hans and Hess, William, *Fighters over Tunisia.* Neville Spearman, 1974

Sturtivant, Ray and Balance, Theo, *Squadrons of the Fleet Air Arm.* Air Britain, 1994

Sturtivant, Ray and Burrow, Mick, *Fleet Air Arm Aircraft 1939-1945.* Air Britain, 1995

ACKNOWLEDGEMENTS

The author wishes to record his gratitude to the following former Hurricane pilots who have given of their time in answering queries and presenting accounts of their actions for inclusion within this volume: Sqn Ldr D H Brocklehurst DFC, Wg Cdr J M V Carpenter DFC, the late Wg Cdr A G Conway DFC, Sqn Ldr M C C Cotton DFC, Wg Cdr E H Dean, Gp Capt T A F Elsdon OBE DFC, Sqn Ldr V K Jacobs, Wg Cdr R F Martin DFC, Sqn Ldr P F Morfill DFM, Sqn Ldr D B F Nichols DFC, Gp Capt J A O'Neil, the late Wg Cdr J G Sanders DFC, Air Cdre J A Sowrey DFC AFC, Wg Cdr A G Todd DFC and Gp Capt R J Walker DSO. The author is also most grateful to the many friends and fellow enthusiasts, too numerous to mention, who have generously given their support to bring this volume to fruition.

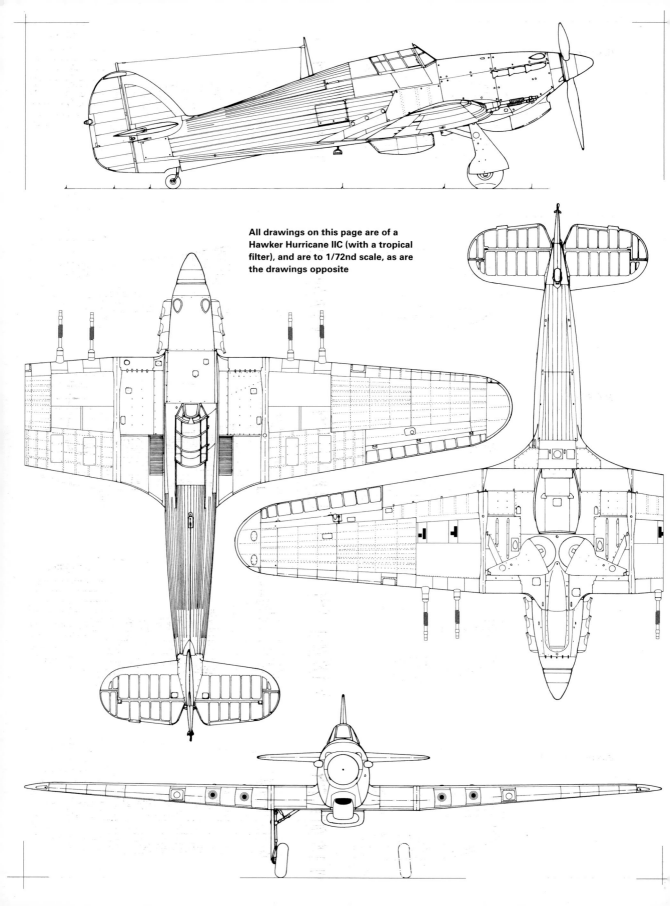

All drawings on this page are of a Hawker Hurricane IIC (with a tropical filter), and are to 1/72nd scale, as are the drawings opposite

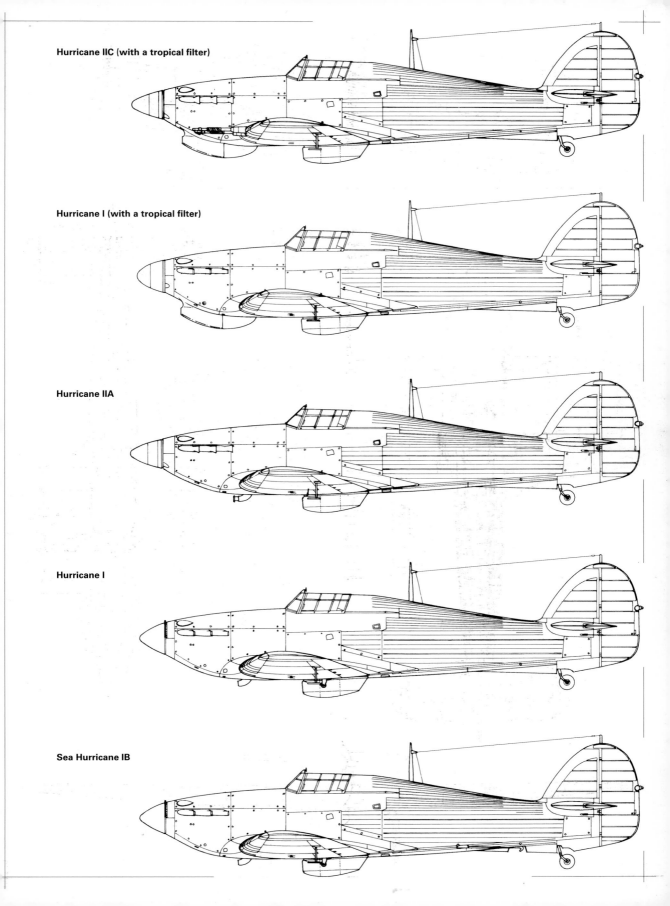

Hurricane IIC (with a tropical filter)

Hurricane I (with a tropical filter)

Hurricane IIA

Hurricane I

Sea Hurricane IB

INDEX

References to illustrations are shown in **bold**. Plates are shown with page and caption locators in (brackets).